JourneyThrough®

Acts

50 Devotional Insights by **David Cook**

Our Daily Bread Publishing.

Requests for permission to quote
from this book should be directed to:
Permissions Department
Our Daily Bread Publishing
PO Box 3566
Grand Rapids, MI 49501
Or contact us by email at permissionsdept@odb.org.

Design by Joshua Tan
Typeset by Grace Goh

ISBN: 978-1-64070-088-8

Printed in the United States of America
23 24 25 26 27 28 29 30 / 9 8 7 6 5 4 3 2

Preface

Former physician and preacher Dr. Martyn Lloyd-Jones once said, "I know of no greater tonic, in the realm of the Spirit, than a thorough reading of that book." He was referring to the book of Acts, and that's good advice coming from a renowned medical doctor.

Luke is the author of both the gospel that bears his name and the book of Acts. Like a modern movie director, he never lets his camera slip out of focus or off target. We might be tempted to follow characters touched by the gospel back to their homes: the Ethiopian treasurer or perhaps the Philippian jailer and his newly Christian family. We would love the camera to linger longer, but it never does. The focus in the gospel is on the Lord Jesus and His movement toward Jerusalem; in Acts, the focus is on the unstoppable gospel as it moves out of Jerusalem and to the ends of the earth.

Let this book be a tonic for you, strengthening your faith in God as you let Him work in and through you to bring the gospel to others. This gospel is still powerful in transforming and bringing people to new life in Christ. The same God is at work, and we are empowered by the same Spirit to bring the same gospel to the world.

All glory to Him,
David Cook

We're glad you've decided to join us on a journey into a deeper relationship with Jesus Christ!

For more than sixty years, we have been known for our devotional booklet, *Our Daily Bread*. Many readers enjoy the encouraging, inspiring, and relevant articles that point them to God and the wisdom and promises of His unchanging Word.

Building on the foundation of *Our Daily Bread*, we have developed this Bible study series to help believers spend time with God in His Word, book by book. We trust that this daily meditation on the Bible will draw you into a closer relationship with Him through our Lord and Savior, Jesus Christ.

How to use this resource

READ: This book is designed to be read alongside God's Word as you journey with Him. It offers explanatory notes to help you understand the Scriptures in fresh ways.

REFLECT: The questions are designed to help you respond to God and the Bible, letting Him change you from the inside out.

RECORD: The space provided allows you to keep a diary of your journey as you record your thoughts and jot down your responses.

An Overview

The book of Acts is one of the most exciting parts of the whole Bible. Jesus has just ascended to heaven, the Spirit has come to the church, and we see God at work. Luke's purpose in writing Acts is to show the triumphant progress of the gospel, starting from Jerusalem, through Judea, into Samaria, throughout Asia Minor, into Europe, and finally to Rome. However, this is not bragging about successes, for the gospel messengers will be opposed, tortured, imprisoned, and martyred. There will be opposition from outside religious and commercial interests and even dissension within the church, yet the gospel will progress and people will come to Christ. Embark on a journey through the book of Acts, and see how the Holy Spirit empowers the church to witness in ever-widening circles until the gospel reaches the ends of the earth (Acts 1:8).

The Structure of Acts

1–7   The gospel in Jerusalem and Judea; Peter the primary apostle; Jews the primary target

8–12   Into Samaria; Peter still active; Paul converted; the Gentile Cornelius converted

13–28   The missionary journeys; the gospel reaches Rome; Paul the primary apostle; Jews still contacted first, but Gentiles now the primary target

Key Verse

"But you will receive power when the Holy Spirit comes on you; and you will be my witnesses in Jerusalem, and in all Judea and Samaria, and to the ends of the earth."
—Acts 1:8

Day 1

Read Luke 24:46–49 and Acts 1:8

Luke is the author of both the gospel of Luke and the book of Acts. Today's verses provide the bridge between the two volumes.

In Luke 24:46–47, Jesus summarizes the purpose of God. Notice that verse 46 is a good summary of Luke's gospel—the suffering, death, and resurrection of the Christ. Verse 47 is a good summary of Acts—that same gospel being preached to the ends of the earth. Also notice that verse 47 is as much the purpose of God as verse 46. It clearly states that the broadcast of the gospel, sometimes called evangelism, is at the very heart of God's ongoing purpose until His Son returns.

Acts 1:8 is a verse similar to Luke 24:47–49. It sets the pattern for the unfolding narrative of Acts. The Holy Spirit will come on the church to empower Christ followers to bear witness in ever-widening circles until the gospel reaches the ends of the earth.

One of the characteristics of Luke's writing is that he allows his emphasis to fall on his last words. In the original Greek, the last word of his long introduction in Luke 1:4 is "certainty." He wants his patron Theophilus to be certain of the facts that Luke reports.

Similarly, in Greek the last words of Acts are "without hindrance" (28:31). The gospel has reached Rome, and it will continue on its unstoppable and unhindered way until all God's purposes have been fulfilled. This truth will be amply demonstrated throughout the book.

The book of Acts provides the church of the twenty-first century with its mandate and your mandate for today. **You have the Holy Spirit. He will empower you today for witness to Christ in a lost world.**

Christian preacher and author C. H. Spurgeon correctly commented, "All hope in ministry lies in the Spirit of God operating on the spirit of men."[1]

1. C. H. Spurgeon, quoted in *Reformation and Revival* 9, no. 1 (2000).

Think of the people
you come in contact
with and of your
witness to them.
How can it be more
effective?

Do you think we
make Luke 24:47 of
lesser importance
than Luke 24:46?
What effect does this
have on the church?

Day 2

Read Acts 1:1–11

The opening two verses connect the reader to Luke 1:1–4, and just as in Luke, they are addressed to Theophilus. Acts takes up where the gospel of Luke left off—that is, with the resurrection of Jesus.

In Acts 1:4–8, Luke records Jesus's final words to His disciples before He ascends to His Father. The disciples' question in verse 6 is a natural one. As resurrected Messiah, will Jesus now bring down the curtain of history, restore Israel to her rightful place, and reign over all creation? Jesus makes it clear that before this happens, there is more to be done; but it is not merely human work, it is Spirit-empowered witness.

So they are to wait (v. 4), and they will receive power (v. 8)—this is the gift of God to His people of which John the Baptist was speaking (v. 5), the baptism of the Holy Spirit. The effect of this baptism is that the Holy Spirit will enable the church in its witness. Your witness today is one part of a two-part witness. You witness, but as you do, the Holy Spirit also witnesses with you (see John 15:26–27).

Jesus then ascends to the right hand of the Father (Acts 1:9; 2:33).

The proof of this, says Peter, is the outpouring of the Holy Spirit (vv. 32–33). The disciples are reminded that just as Jesus has gone up, so He will come down. These heavenly messengers, similar to those who announced the resurrection (Luke 24:4), now remind the church that Jesus, who has just ascended, will come back again (Acts 1:10–11). This implies a limited time to work until Jesus returns.

Jesus spoke of His ascension in Luke 22:69. **His resurrection culminated in His ascension, and His ascension means His total exaltation to the right hand of God where He intercedes for us (Romans 8:34).** He now occupies the highest place (Philippians 2:9). He bestows gifts to His people (Ephesians 4:11), and from the place of exaltation, He will return in triumph to bring in the new heaven and the new earth.

It is little wonder that Paul encourages us to set our hearts and minds on the things above, where Christ is seated at God's right hand (Colossians 3:1–3).

Think of the ways in which Christ's ascension can be a source of blessing for you. What is He doing at the Father's right hand?

What do you think the ascension meant to the Lord Jesus?

Day 3

Read Acts 1:12–26

With the final separation of Jesus from His disciples, now numbering 120 (Acts 1:15), one would have expected gloom to set in. But no, we find the Christians going about their business. They return to Jerusalem where Jesus told them they were to wait for the gift of God (v. 4), and they set themselves to pray earnestly (v. 14).

Peter seems by now to be the acknowledged leader and spokesman for the group. He sees, in the betrayal of Christ by Judas and the selection of a replacement for him among the apostles, a fulfillment of Psalms 69:25 and 109:8. To qualify for selection, a man must have been with the apostles from the time John was baptizing up to the ascension of Jesus. Also, he must have personally seen the risen Christ, as a witness to the resurrection (Acts 1:21–22). Two men are proposed, prayer is offered for guidance, lots are cast, and Matthias is added to the eleven apostles.

Why does Luke include this detail? Why not move from the ascension straight to Pentecost? After all, Matthias is not mentioned again in the book. The betrayal by Judas demonstrated his failure as a leader, and that situation had to be acknowledged and rectified. Luke tells us in some detail of the failure of Judas because he is providing a "warts and all" coverage of the history of the church. He does not idealize the church; he recognizes the hypocrisy of Ananias and Sapphira in Acts 5, the bickering over the widows in Acts 6, Peter's behavior in Acts 10, and even Paul's impatience with John Mark in Acts 15.

"The best of men are men at best." **We are to recognize our own frailty, and Luke shows the church facing up to the need to renew its leadership following the apostasy of one of the apostles.** Damage had been done, and restoration was required. The church did not—and must not—simply try to cover up its sin. Sin needs to be acknowledged and dealt with.

In an atmosphere of prayer, Peter sets out the necessary criteria, the lot is cast, and Matthias is the choice. The apostolate is now complete once more, and its key function is to witness to the reality of Christ's resurrection (1:22).

Bible commentator Matthew Henry said of verse 22, "See what the apostles were ordained to; not a secular dignity and dominion . . . but to preach Christ and the power of His resurrection."[2]

2. Matthew Henry, *Commentary on the Whole Bible*, vol. 6 (McLean, VA: MacDonald, 1985).

In what ways does the early church provide a model for us concerning leadership selection?

In what ways does the example of Judas serve as a warning to you (vv. 16–17)?

Day 4

Read Acts 2:1–13

Pentecost (meaning "fifty") was one of the three great festivals of Judaism, known as the Festival of Weeks in the Old Testament (Deuteronomy 16:9–12). Celebrated fifty days after the beginning of barley harvest, it was a time to give thanks to God for the completion of the harvest. Later, it came to commemorate the giving of the law to Moses at Mount Sinai (Exodus 19:1). The festival was all about fulfillment, completion, and finality. It is most fitting then that the Holy Spirit should be poured out on the church at this festival. His coming is the evidence that Christ has risen and ascended to God's right hand; His work is now complete.

The coming of the Spirit is associated with the sound of wind (Acts 2:2; see John 3:8) and the sight of fire (Acts 2:3; see Exodus 3:2). The effect is that the 120 gathered disciples were filled with the Holy Spirit (Acts 2:4; see Jeremiah 31:33, which anticipates this day) and they speak in tongues, so the different language groups in the crowd (Acts 2:9–11) hear them disclosing the wonders of God in their own language. Luke records the range of responses—"bewilderment" (v. 6), "utterly amazed" (v. 7), "amazed and perplexed" (v. 12), and mockery (v. 13).

Note that the recipients did not speak in inarticulate sounds. The word "language" in verse 6 translates the original word "dialect" and parallels with verses 4 and 11 where the word used is *glossa*, or tongue. The ideas are parallel, and the words are used synonymously—the "tongue" here is a dialect. Here are people speaking in known native languages and dialects without having attended language school.

The focus of these verses is that God has come to live among His people, and according to some commentaries, the immediate effect of this is the reversal of the scrambling of languages that occurred with the building of the Tower of Babel (Genesis 11). **The Holy Spirit has come upon the church, and He enables effective witness.** He is the Spirit who Jesus said would empower believers for witness (Acts 1:8).

Matthew Henry says the significance of this event "is to dignify and so to distinguish these men as messengers from heaven and therefore like Moses at the bush, the crowd will turn aside and see this great sight."[3]

3. Henry, *Commentary on the Whole Bible.*

How do you think
the Holy Spirit helps
you in your witness?

What do you think
wind, fire, and
tongues might
symbolize about the
Holy Spirit's ministry?

Day 5

Read Acts 2:14–41

Whenever a crowd gathers in Acts, a believer takes the opportunity of preaching to it. Here is Peter, who a little earlier had denied Christ, now fearlessly preaching the gospel with crystal clarity. In our era, the day of Pentecost is the day in the church calendar when many churches preach on the Holy Spirit. But the Spirit is not the focus of Peter's address; rather, Jesus is. Peter speaks only of the Spirit in relation to Jesus.

The big idea of this Pentecostal sermon is that Jesus was crucified, was raised to life, and was exalted at God's right hand, and that Peter and the others are eyewitnesses of these events. Jesus was accredited by God (Acts 2:22) according to the set purpose of God, was crucified (v. 23), and was raised from the dead. Death had no claim on Him because He had no sin (v. 24). The proof that He is exalted to God's right hand is that He now pours out the Holy Spirit (vv. 32–33). The summary is found in verse 36.

Peter's audience was Jewish. Therefore, he wants them to know that they should not be surprised at these events because they fulfill what Joel predicted for the last days (vv. 17–21;

Joel 2:28–32). In Acts 2:25–28, Peter quotes David in Psalm 16:8–11. Acts 2:27 contains rich and highly significant words—Peter says David did not use these words of himself but of one greater than David who will not be abandoned "to the realm of the dead." The Old Testament is Peter's reference point for the Jewish audience.

Notice also that Peter does not hesitate to be direct. In verses 23–24, he makes the clearest contrast between what they did to the Son— "put him to death"—and what God himself did—"raised him from the dead." The response to this sermon was deep conviction (v. 37). Peter tells his listeners they are to repent and give public witness to their repentance through baptism (v. 38). **The Christian gospel involves take-and-give (v. 38). God takes our sin and deals with it and then gives us His Holy Spirit.** This is the ongoing offer to all those who repent and turn to Christ.

Three thousand people accepted the message that day (v. 41).

Think about the twin blessings of forgiveness and the Holy Spirit you have received. Turn your thoughts into praise.

In verse 40, Luke describes Peter as warning the crowd. Are we serious enough in sharing the gospel with others?

Day 6

Read Acts 2:42–47

One of the features of modern culture is our intense population density, yet we lack togetherness. We often have proximity without community.

In these verses, we read of the community life of the prototype church. They shared the common experience of hearing the gospel, repenting, and being baptized. They also shared a common devotion (the idea of the word is "attachment like glue"). They stuck to the apostolic teaching and to the community, to the breaking of bread and prayer. The "breaking of bread" may indicate the Lord's Supper.

Jesus prayed in John 17:20–23 for the complete unity of believers. We now see this deep unity built around a common experience and common devotion.

This even extended to a Spirit-motivated voluntary generosity (Acts 2:44–45). We may think that the church was fairly self-absorbed, but no, their pooling of resources was to meet human need. At a time when the government was not concerned for social welfare, and when life was cutthroat and cheap, it is no wonder

that people were impressed with this new society growing up in their midst in Jerusalem, "enjoying the favor of all the people" (v. 47).

Again Luke reminds us that this impressive community is not just a matter of people turning over a new leaf, but it is superintended by God (v. 43). God enabled the apostles to do wonders and "the Lord added to their number" (v. 47). This is God at work through the life and witness of His people.

The church is never to be a closed, secret, and introverted community. All true fellowship is founded upon and focused on the gospel. **All true fellowship overflows into evangelism, which after all is the overarching mandate of the church (1:8).**

You need such a fellowship with your fellow believers. The fractured world needs to see church communities witnessing to the reality of substantially restored human relationships because of the gospel.

How can you encourage your local fellowship to be more like its prototype?

Note how often community words are used in verses 42–47. How does this idea challenge our unhealthy individualism?

Day 7

Read Acts 3:1–10

The apostles did many miraculous signs (Acts 2:43). Today we read of Peter healing a lame beggar.

In such a dynamic book that shows the gospel "on the move," it's ironic that the first sign should concern an immobile man. This man was obviously totally dependent, having to be carried to the temple to beg. Another irony is that a man in such desperate need should be placed at the gate called Beautiful (3:2). He was now over forty years old (4:22), and he had been crippled since birth (3:2). All the world could do for him was to throw a few coins his way. Peter and John, however, were clear that Jesus could do far more.

Peter has no coins to give him. Rather, he calls on him in the name of Jesus Christ of Nazareth to walk (v. 6). The response is instantaneous. It is not that he got better gradually; his feet and ankles immediately became strong so that he went walking and jumping (vv. 7–8). This is an incredible creation miracle, removing the cause of paralysis and bringing muscle into existence. Even the Sanhedrin could not deny the reality of "a notable sign" (4:16).

It is clear that just as God had accredited Jesus by miracles and signs (2:22) so He is now accrediting the apostles, and therefore their message, in the same way (14:3).

The crowd is filled with wonder and amazement (3:10). Peter takes the opportunity afforded by the gathering of a crowd to preach the gospel to them. **The church is mandated to preach the gospel. The sign both draws a crowd to hear the gospel and authenticates the message.**

Peter, the source of Mark's gospel, would have remembered Jesus's words from Mark 1:38 when the crowd was looking for Him to heal: He told them that He had come to preach. "That is why I have come." The healing of the man was a means of solving his deeper need as well as that of the crowd—to become eternally healthy.

In what ways is the beggar's physical experience symbolic of our spiritual experience?

Is there ground here to think that the church's mandate is to preach and heal?

Day 8

Read Acts 3:11–26

One distinctive feature about the preaching of the apostles is their obvious self-effacement. Politicians like Herod may bask in self-glorification with disastrous results (Acts 12:21–23), but the apostles are the very opposite (14:11–15). The apostles are not gurus seeking the limelight and the acclamation of the crowds. So Peter makes it clear it is not because of his and John's power or godliness that the paralyzed man walks; it's because of Jesus (3:16).

Again, a clear distinction is stated between how the Jews treated Jesus—they disowned (vv. 13–14) and killed Him (v. 15), no doubt thinking they were acting consistently with their traditions and orthodoxy—and how God treated Jesus. God glorified Him (v. 13) and raised Him (v. 15), and the apostles were eyewitnesses to this. Peter calls for a response in verses 17–26, highlighting the strong Jewish heritage of Christ and how all that has happened is in fulfillment of the Old Testament Scriptures (see vv. 18, 21–25).

God is in control. God is working out His purposes. Therefore the Jewish crowd is to repent, for they have the privilege of being heirs to the promises of God (v. 25).

Their repentance will bring about forgiveness and times of refreshing, including, in Peter's mind, the return of Christ as He had promised (vv. 19–20). Christ's return from heaven will be the ultimate fulfillment of God's promises to restore all things at His coming (v. 21).

Peter sees Jesus as the fulfillment of God's promises to Moses in Deuteronomy 18:15–19:

- Like Moses, Jesus is from among their own.

- God will put His words in Jesus's mouth.

- God will call those who disobey Jesus to account.

Jesus is the prophet who not only speaks God's words but also is God's Word (John 1:14, 18). When Jesus speaks, God speaks. When Jesus acts, God acts. In Jesus's attitudes, we see the attitudes of God.

The healing of a paralyzed man is God accrediting His Son and His words. It is little wonder that Israel should repent of their disobedience and their treatment of Him, as should we.

How much is ongoing repentance toward God part of your daily experience?

How does apostolic self-effacement challenge self-exalting spiritual leadership?

Day 9

Read Acts 4:1–12

The world is no friend of God's church. Today we meet a theme in Acts that will repeat itself throughout the book—opposition.

The concern of the Jewish authorities is seen in Acts 4:2, the "proclaiming in Jesus the resurrection of the dead." Luke is quick to remind us that in spite of opposition the gospel continues on its all-conquering way (v. 4). The same people who called for the crucifixion of Jesus now question Peter and John as to how they performed this miracle (vv. 5–7).

Peter is both clear and courageous in his answer. It is Jesus who is responsible for the miracle. "Jesus Christ of Nazareth, whom you crucified but whom God raised from the dead" (v. 10), and this was to fulfill Psalm 118:22, that the one rejected would ultimately triumph (Acts 4:11).

Here again is the familiar pattern of evangelism to the Jewish audience:

- The contrast of what you did and what God did

- The death and resurrection of Jesus

- The fulfillment of the Scriptures

Acts 4:12 is a timely reminder to us of the uniqueness of Christ. There is no other who can save—"no one else . . . no other name." Such a verse makes it clear that Christ is the only way to God. The basis of such a claim is that He is the one who died, was raised, and was exalted to God's right hand. Further proof as to the reality of the claim is the paralyzed man standing healed before them. The ascended Christ is still active.

When John the Baptist doubted whether Jesus was the Christ, he asked the right question: "Are you the one who is to come, or should we expect someone else?" (Matthew 11:3). If Jesus is not the way, or not the sole way, who else has done what He did? Should we still be looking for another? The answer of the gospel is, "no one else . . . no other name."

Peter and John are accused, they are being interrogated, but they are not passive victims. They are on the front foot; they are on the attack with the gospel.

ThinkThrough

Memorize Acts 4:12 and think about its implications for you, your friends, the world, and evangelism.

How should you respond in the face of opposition to the gospel?

Day 10

Read Acts 4:13–22

In John 7:15, the Jews were amazed that Jesus knew so much without ever having studied. In today's passage, the Jewish leaders are amazed at the courage of Peter and John, who speak authoritatively despite their lack of formal religious training, and they note that "these men had been with Jesus" (Acts 4:13).

We are amazed at the blindness of the Sanhedrin, that despite the clear evidence of the healing of the man and the claim that this was the work of Jesus, they may have thought they could stop the gospel by making a motion in the assembly that there should be no more Jesus talk. There is no rational debate or presentation of contrary evidence, merely this response—"speak no longer to anyone in this name" (v. 17). Perhaps they thought this would change reality and everything would go back to the way it was. No way! Peter and John had been with Jesus. They had "seen and heard" (v. 20) and were eyewitnesses of His resurrection and exaltation. They are under the authority of God, who is an even higher authority than the Sanhedrin (v. 19). They will maintain their position in Acts 5:29. Let the highest court of Judaism decide—should God be obeyed or a human court?

The Jewish leadership had often opposed Roman interference in their customs. They claimed that their ultimate authority was no human court, but God alone. Peter and John had the same conviction. They were witnesses, and they had been with Jesus. They were the leaders of a group of people mandated by God himself to speak. "We cannot help speaking" (v. 20), they say, so they give us the ongoing model for our response to human-centered opposition that seeks to silence our speaking of the gospel.

What the prophet heard, "thus says the Lord," the apostles saw and heard, and so spoke. **Today we can say with equal confidence, "thus the Lord has written."** We have the historical written record of the revelation of God and the accredited testimony of the prophets and the apostles, both of which focus on the Lord Jesus, and so we must speak. The more determined the world is to ignore us, the more determined we must be to speak out of love, compassion, and the truths of God's Word.

Think of the fear you have for the tribunal compared with the fear you have for God. How could Peter and John have had such courage?

In the face of such clear evidence, why does the Sanhedrin refuse to recognize the truth?

Day 11

Read Acts 4:23–31

The immediate response of the church to the threats of the chief priests and elders is to pray. They do not try political maneuvering, and they do not ask for safety. They pray to the Sovereign Lord (Acts 4:24), reminding themselves that it is God who is in control, not the Sanhedrin. They remind themselves that He is the Sovereign Creator. They remind themselves of the Scriptures, of Psalm 2:1–2—all of humankind's raging and plotting against God's Anointed One is in vain (Acts 4:25).

Again, in verse 27, they mention the human players, but in verse 28, they put them in their place. Herod, Pontius Pilate, the Gentiles, and the people of Israel conspired against Jesus, but they could only do what God had decided beforehand should be allowed to happen. As Joseph reminded his brothers in Genesis 50:20, "You intended to harm me, but God intended it for good." Here is the crowning conviction of Romans 8:28—that in all things God works for the good of His people, and in all things God will take the evil intentions of people and use them to accomplish His purpose. The cross is the best example of that.

The mandate of the church is to speak the gospel, and the church prays that it would do so (Acts 4:29–30)—that no threat will slow down the church in its ministry. Note again that they do not pray for safety but for bold speech (v. 29) and accredited speech (v. 30). Luke records the shaking of the place and their filling with the Holy Spirit; the same believers who had been baptized in the Spirit are influenced afresh by Him. We are baptized once but enabled by the Spirit always.

The fruit of the Spirit's presence is again underlined in verse 31— allowing bold speaking of the Word of God. **The first resort of the church under threat of persecution is to pray about God's sovereign control; its petition is about bold speech; and the result is spiritual fullness showing itself in bold gospel proclamation.**

This is a great pattern for us today who are under all kinds of threats to have our message marginalized and diminished.

How does this experience of the church show you the best way to face up to a tough situation?

Are you facing a similar situation today? If so, then write out a prayer similar to that of the first-century church and pray it in relation to your situation.

Day 12

Read Acts 4:32–37

Again, as in Acts 2:42–47, Luke gives us a glimpse of life in the early church, and what an impressive community it is!

Life in the first century could be difficult. There was little public welfare. People often had only their own family networks, and if those failed, they were on their own. The unity of the Christian community extended to possessions; they shared everything as if they were members of one family. The principle was one of equality. If a person or a family was needy, their needs were met by the abundance of others, who sold their possessions and laid the money at the apostles' feet for distribution (Acts 4:34). Here, then, is a Spirit-inspired generosity. Soviet leader Nikita Khrushchev once said that communism's downfall was its failure to produce the selfless man. **What the political system cannot do, God can do through the gospel of His Son. Here is a selfless, generous community of people of the new covenant.**

Luke mentions one person as an example, Joseph of Cyprus. Renamed Barnabas, the son of encouragement, by the apostles, he did what was described in verses 34–35. True to his name, Barnabas introduces Saul to the apostles in Jerusalem at a time when the other believers were hesitant to accept their former persecutor (9:26–27). Barnabas is sent by the church in Jerusalem to encourage the Gentile church in Antioch (11:22–24) and goes to Tarsus to invite Paul to participate (v. 25). He leads the first missionary journey with Paul (13:2). Paul soon becomes the dominant partner, and Barnabas willingly plays second fiddle (13:42, 46; 14:1, 12). Barnabas was far more patient and generous-minded toward Mark than Paul was (15:36–41). Barnabas is a great example of humility and generosity. He was a true disciple of Christ, and he came to serve (Mark 10:45).

I pray a daily prayer that God would give me a mind that is clean, generous, and humble. Barnabas is a very good example of a life lived with such a mind. But Luke will not have us idealize the early church, because the generosity of Barnabas stands out in stark contrast to what is about to follow in Acts 5.

ThinkThrough

What is it about Barnabas that gives you a model to follow today?

What changes might the principle of equality bring about in your fellowship? Do you think our responsibilities toward fellow believers have an economic aspect as well?

Day 13

Read Acts 5:1–11

Today we meet sin for the first time in the new covenant community.

When Israel entered the promised land, God showed with His judgment of Achan's sin (Joshua 7) how seriously He takes this subject. Now God shows His new covenant community the unacceptability of sin.

God's judgment on Ananias (v. 5) and his wife Sapphira (v. 10) was instantaneous. What they had done was devil-inspired (v. 3) and constituted lying to the Holy Spirit (v. 3), lying to God (v. 4), and testing the Spirit of the Lord (v. 9). What precisely was their sin? They had conspired together to sell a piece of property, like Barnabas, and they lay only a portion of the sale price at the apostles' feet as if it were the whole amount. Perhaps they wanted a reputation for generosity like Barnabas had—while keeping back part of the money for themselves.

It was this deception that Peter highlights (v. 4). It was their land and they could have kept all of the money for themselves, but they appeared to want a reputation that was built on deception. If so, they hypocritically wanted an undeserved reputation. Whether or not Ananias and Sapphira were true Christians is not answered, although they were certainly part of the new covenant community. In his New Testament commentary on Acts, Simon Kistemaker concluded, "The divisive intervention to stop deceit within the early church strikes fear in the hearts of every member of the church."

What an impression the quick judgment of Ananias and Sapphira must have made on the young men referred to in verses 6 and 10. They may have wondered when all this was going to stop. A primary sin of the religious leaders of Jesus's day hypocrisy (Matthew 23:3); teaching one thing yet doing another. It is this sin that enters the Christian community and is judged.

Beware of disguising who you really are, of seeking a reputation that does not fit with the reality of your life.

In what ways may hypocrisy show itself in your life today?

Why might this incident, extreme as it seems, represent the mercy of God?

Day 14

Read Acts 5:12–41

Despite external persecution and internal hypocrisy, the church continues to grow.

Clearly God is accrediting His gospel message in miraculous ways (Acts 5:15–16). Luke now tells us that the motivation of the high priest and his associates is jealousy (v. 17), the same motivation behind their earlier attitude toward Jesus (Matthew 27:18). But prison is an ineffective weapon against the apostles. God's messengers cannot be stopped as long as He has work for them to do.

The Jewish religious authorities did not like the apostles' claim that they were responsibile for the death of Jesus (Acts 5:28). Verses 29–32 are an excellent summary of the apostolic response. Note the following elements:

- God raised Jesus from the dead, though you killed Him on the tree (v. 30).

- God exalted Jesus to His right hand that He might give repentance and forgiveness to Israel (v. 31).

- We are witnesses of this and so is the Holy Spirit (v. 32).

The response to such a message (v. 33) is similar to the response to Stephen's speech later (7:54), and perhaps the apostles would also have met Stephen's fate (see vv. 54–60), but for the wise intercession of Gamaliel (5:34–39). Gamaliel reminds the Sanhedrin of Theudas (v. 36) and Judas the Galilean (v. 37), both rose up as leaders and drew a following but were later killed, their followers scattering. Similarly, he says, let the apostles go, for their cause will fail if it is of human origin (v. 38). If, on the other hand, it is of God, then who can effectively oppose it (v. 39)?

The apostles are flogged and then released, but they keep teaching and proclaiming, despite the Sanhedrin forbidding that activity. Saul (who will be known as Paul after his conversion), though a student of Gamaliel (22:3), had no such open attitude to Christianity. He saw that the old system must stay; therefore, the new must be banished.

According to the logic of Gamaliel, the ongoing growth of the church and its continuation to this day is ample evidence of its divine origin. **To oppose the gospel is to fight against God (5:39), surely a hopeless enterprise.**

Why did Gamaliel and Saul have such different attitudes to the new movement?

What emotions are evident in those who oppose the apostles (see vv. 17, 24, 26, 33)?

Day 15

Read Acts 6:1–7

Luke continues with his realistic portrayal of the Christian community. At this stage, the early church consisted of believing Jews both from a Hebrew-speaking background as well as from a Greek-speaking background. The Greek-speaking Jews complained that their widows were being discriminated against in the daily distribution of the welfare, which favored Hebrew-speaking widows.

In Acts 6:2, the apostolic response is both swift and public. They recognize the priority of their own ministry, "the word of God." But they are not implying that the ministry of the table (that is, distributing food) is beneath them, because they show that this is a ministry to be undertaken by men "full of the Spirit and wisdom" (v. 3).

The apostles gladly delegate this serving ministry so they can focus on prayer and the word, which is their key ministry. The good is the enemy of the best. Thank God that the apostles recognized God's call to the best in their own ministry of the word and prayer, and they made sure it was not disrupted by the good that is waiting on tables.

The whole community (v. 5) chose seven men who they set apart for this ministry (v. 6). In a community culturally divided like the early church, there is great sensitivity to the potential disruption, which could flow from the complaint that the Greek-speaking widows were being overlooked (v. 1). Seven men, all having Greek names, were chosen; not five Greek-speakers to two Hebrew-speakers, or four to three, but seven Greek-speakers to nil.

This shows the early church's determination "to keep the unity of the Spirit through the bond of peace" (Ephesians 4:3). The apostles' clear thinking and their commitment to this God-given unity is blessed by God. The result (Acts 6:7) is the rapid increase of the church, with the gospel reaching deeply into Judaism and a large number of priests becoming believers. The gospel continues on its march to the ends of the earth. The threat of prison, and now internal dissent, does not frustrate its progress.

What can we learn about handling disruptions in the local church by what the apostles do here?

How does the apostolic conviction evidenced here encourage you in your ministry?

Day 16

Read Acts 6:8–15

The focus now shifts to one of the seven chosen men, who is described in Acts 6:3 as "full of the Spirit and wisdom" and in verse 8 as "full of God's grace and power."

Luke gives a great deal of space to Stephen because his martyrdom will be the catalyst (see 8:1; 11:19) for the spread of the gospel to non-Jewish, Gentile territory. Greek-speaking Jews begin to argue with Stephen (Acts 6:9), but when they cannot better him in argument, they resort to underhanded ways. They persuade some men to make false allegations about Stephen and have him brought before the Sanhedrin. The allegations (v. 11) charge him with blaspheming against Moses and God. This is elaborated in verses 13–14 with the claim that Stephen speaks against the temple and the law, teaching that Jesus will destroy the former and change the latter.

In many ways the experience of Stephen parallels the experience of Jesus Christ; see the similar charge made against Jesus in Matthew 26:61 and Mark 14:57. The best false charges are those with an element of truth. Stephen probably did report Christ as speaking of the destruction of the temple (meaning His body), of the fulfillment of the law, and in favor of the new covenant gospel.

Stephen's composure and serenity are obvious (Acts 6:15). He is now ready to answer the charges before the highest court of Judaism—the Sanhedrin. When reasoned debate fails (as in Acts 4 with the Sanhedrin and Acts 6 with the Synagogue of the Freedmen), people often resort either to the oppressive exercise of power or the desperate search for fake witnesses and charges in order to impose silence.

For the Christian, however, the best case for truth is made by its clear and open presentation. God is the great evangelist who blesses the clear proclamation of truth. Like Paul, we renounce underhanded ways that seek to manipulate adherence to the gospel (2 Corinthians 4:2). These methods are unworthy of the gospel itself. Our trust is not in eloquence, but in God to do His work through the gospel (1 Corinthians 2:1). Neither is our interest in quelling the rights of others to proclaim their religion, for truth has nothing to fear from its counterfeits.

The opposition of the ungodly to the gospel is stubborn, irrational, and perverse. Satan "has blinded the minds of unbelievers, so that they cannot see the light of the gospel"

(2 Corinthians 4:4). Like Stephen and Paul, our response must be to preach not ourselves, "but Jesus Christ as Lord" (v. 5).

ThinkThrough

How inevitable is opposition for the faithful Christian witness?

How irrational is the world's opposition to the gospel today? Does it still respond underhandedly?

Day 17

Read Acts 7:1–53

Stephen's speech in Acts 7 to the Sanhedrin, the highest court of Judaism, falls into three sections:

• Verses 2–16: The Patriarchs, Abraham, Isaac, and Jacob—God's presence in Israel's history

• Verses 17–43: Moses and the law, dealing with the charge of blaspheming against Moses

• Verses 44–50: The temple and the charge of blaspheming against God

Stephen reviews Israel's history to demonstrate that Israel has always rejected God's messengers, culminating in the murder of God's righteous one (v. 52). Similar histories are found in Psalms 78 and 107. Here is an outline of Stephen's history in Acts 7:

• Verses 2–16 recount God's covenantal relationship with Israel's patriarchs, and yet even here there is rejection of Joseph (v. 9).

• Verses 17–43 recall where the Israelites rejected Moses (vv. 27–29) and turned their backs on him, making the golden calf (v. 41). Stephen is being accused of blasphemy of Moses, yet Israel's history is one of rejection of Moses (v. 39).

• Verses 44–50 relate to the place of worship. Although Solomon built God's temple (v. 47), the idea of God being tied to a place is never taught

in Scripture (vv. 49–50). The whole world is God's temple (Isaiah 66:1–2), and Solomon himself said as much (2 Chronicles 6:18). By attaching excessive importance to a man-made temple, Stephen's accusers are resisting the Holy Spirit (Acts 7:51) and rejecting God's prophetic word of the change to come.

Stephen makes it clear that God cannot be localized. He was with Abraham in Mesopotamia (v. 2), with Joseph in Egypt (v. 9), and with Moses at Mount Sinai (v. 30). He could not be limited to a calf, a tabernacle, or a temple—He is the pilgrim God.

As to blasphemy against Moses, the nation has always been guilty of that. As to blasphemy against God, Israel has not only localized God to the temple but, at the same time, has rejected God's true temple, the Lord Jesus. It is in Him that God and people meet.

Stephen condemns the Jews as being like the pagans—stubborn, resistant, and unrepentant (v. 51). They have consistently rejected God's messengers, despite the advantage of receiving God's law (vv. 52–53). This is supposed to be a speech by the defense, just as Peter and John were before the Sanhedrin (Acts 4), Stephen is on the attack. His accusers are the ones being accused.

Why does Luke give so much space to the speech? Probably for two reasons: First, the death of Stephen marks the beginning of a series of events that will result in a major advance of the gospel to Gentile lands. Second, we see a model defense of Christianity in the face of Jewish antagonism.

In what ways is the experience of Stephen, the church's first martyr, like that of Christ?

In verse 42, God "gave them over" (see also Romans 1:24, 26, 28). Does God still deal with people the way He dealt with Israel as told in Acts 7:39–43?

Day 18

Read Acts 7:54–8:1

In Acts 2:37, we see deep conviction come upon those who hear Peter's sermon. Stephen's speech also arouses a deep feeling. But it was resentment (7:54), not repentance. Stephen pulls no punches (vv. 51–52). His manner and content is not that of a man looking for acquittal. Yet again we are told by Luke of Stephen's fullness in the Spirit in verse 55, as we were previously told in Acts 6:5 and 8.

Stephen inflames the situation further by claiming to see the Son of Man standing at the right hand of God (7:56). To the Jews, identifying Jesus, a mere man, as the Messiah (Son of Man) was clearly blasphemous, for God is one. So, out of control with rage, they rush to stone him (vv. 57–58). Jesus had ascended to sit at God's right hand (2:34). Here He stands to welcome His first martyr into heaven.

Luke now introduces one of the main characters of his narrative, Saul (7:58; 8:1). He will become better known by his Roman name, Paul (13:9). Saul has clearly heard Stephen and approves of what is happening. As the crowd casts the first stones, they leave their cloaks in Saul's care. Stephen is very much like the Lord Jesus in death—"receive my spirit" (7:59; see Luke 23:46), "do not hold this sin against them" (Acts 7:60; see Luke 23:34). Was Stephen's prayer effective? In the case of Saul, it was!

The focus in the narrative now begins to shift, for God's gospel is on the move—from Jerusalem to Samaria, from Jew to semi-Jew and then to Gentile, from Jerusalem to Antioch, and from Peter to Paul.

Change is a constant for the Christian. **But the gospel never changes, though it is always on the move, conquering lives wherever it goes.** Even through the suffering and pain of its carriers, it continues on in triumph, as we shall see in Acts 8. God uses the death of Stephen to fling His messengers farther out toward the ends of the earth. He is the sovereign God who will glorify himself through our lives and even through our deaths.

Why do you think the Jews of the Sanhedrin were so angry with Stephen?

Why does the death of the apostle James (12:2) get such a brief mention compared with the death of one of the seven chosen men, Stephen (7:54–60)?

Day 19

Read Acts 8:1–13

The early Christian, Tertullian, said, "The blood of the martyrs is the seed of the church."[4] The church scatters out from Jerusalem (Acts 8:1; 11:19), and Saul initiates a thorough search for believers (8:3). There is nothing here of the open-mindedness of Gamaliel (5:33–40).

The body of Stephen was treated with respect, and his loss was keenly felt (8:2).

One of those who was scattered was Philip. He went to the city of Samaria. Through God's blessing, great joy came to the city. **It is significant that Christian repentance is a turning from sin and a turning to God.** In Athens they turn away from idols (17:34), and in Ephesus they abandon superstitious sorcery (19:19). The "turning from" may vary. Here the people turn away from the flashy and spectacular magic offered by Simon and turn to the Lord Jesus and all that is involved in His kingdom (8:12). The gospel of Jesus Christ is what changes people.

Even Simon the sorcerer—astonished by what he saw—believed and was baptized (v. 13). (The Samaritans had an unusual experience of the Spirit, dealt with in tomorrow's reading).

Simon's motivation for gaining the Spirit, however, is apparently commercial. In verse 18 he offers to pay for the Holy Spirit. He is a reminder to us that not all who profess faith and are baptized are truly converted. A person can look good, have all the trappings, and still be full of bitterness and captive to sin (v. 23)! Simon's problem was that he understood neither the nature of Jesus's messiahship nor the person and role of the Holy Spirit. He thought of both as spiritual forces that could be used to gain control of people and make money, a common attitude of the world to "the force" of Christianity.

God is about to authenticate true faith in the Samaritan believers (vv. 14–17), but at the same time, Peter chastises someone for duplicity (vv. 20–23). Peter is exercising this ministry of authentication and exposure, and he is displaying the authority Jesus gave him in Matthew 16:19.

4. Tertullian, quoted in "Apology" 50.14 (Grand Rapids, MI: Eerdmans, 1992).

How did Simon the sorcerer's unregenerate heart show itself?

Simon sought commercial value from the Holy Spirit (vv. 18–24). Why is Peter's response appropriate?

Day 20

Read Acts 8:14–25

Today's passage has been the source of much controversy in the church. Peter and John are sent by the apostles to Samaria, they lay hands on the disciples who have previously been baptized in Jesus's name (Acts 8:16), and they receive the Holy Spirit (v. 17). Whose name should they have been baptized with in order to receive this Holy Spirit? It is clear they were true believers. So why had they not received the Holy Spirit at the time of their repentance, as did the three thousand in Acts 2 and others elsewhere?

Some find here, in this two-stage experience, the basis for the practice of confirmation. That is, through the hand of the confirming bishop, those confirmed receive the Holy Spirit. Others argue that the normal Christian experience is two-stage: conversion is followed by Spirit baptism as a subsequent, second experience. Though other passages in Acts are cited to prove this point, the Acts 8 incident seems the clearest.

Why was there a two-stage experience for the Samaritans when for the rest God forgives our sin and gives us the Holy Spirit at one time (2:38–39)? Should Christians seek further fullness of the Holy Spirit beyond their conversion, thinking that without this second blessing they have not received all God intended for them? There is no evidence of any of the New Testament letters commanding believers to seek such a second blessing. Without such a command from the letters of the New Testament, how then can we explain this two-stage blessing at Samaria?

There was mutual hostility between Jews and Samaritans, and such tension was not to be tolerated in the church.
Perhaps Samaritan believers needed to realize that they were not a separate sect within Christianity. So they received the Holy Spirit through the hands of the Jerusalem apostles. They are part of the one body of Christ. It was also important for Jerusalem believers to know that Samaritan believers were not inferior; the same Holy Spirit filled each. So Peter and John were eyewitnesses of the integrity of the Samaritan believers' experience.

There are so many characters, stories, and experiences of salvation in Acts. But Luke is merely describing a unique experience of the Samaritans here. He is not prescribing a normative spiritual experience for today.

Do people still
desire the Spirit?
How do we receive
the Spirit according
to Acts 2:38–39 and
19:1–6?

Read Ephesians
1:13–14. What
elements make up
the normal Christian
experience?

Day 21

Read Acts 8:26–40

So far we have read of large numbers of people coming to repentance and faith in Jesus (see Acts 2:41, 47; 4:4; 6:7). Now we meet just one man, who highlights God's interest in each and every person.

Philip is directed by an angel to the desert road that goes down from Jerusalem to Gaza. He meets an Ethiopian on his way home from Jerusalem, reading the scrolls of Isaiah. The Spirit directs Philip to the man's chariot (8:29), and Philip asks the Ethiopian if he understands what he is reading. The man invites Philip into the chariot and asks him to explain Isaiah 53:7–8 (Acts 8:31–34). Philip explains that Isaiah is referring to Jesus (v. 35). Verse 37, which appears in many translations, quotes the Ethiopian as saying, "I believe that Jesus Christ is the Son of God" (NASB). The man is baptized, and Philip is taken away by the Spirit of the Lord (vv. 36–39).

The great evangelist of Acts is God himself. His angel gives Philip His direction. He prepares the Ethiopian, who happens to be reading the messianic passage of Isaiah 53. He appoints him to hear the message. He ordains his response (see Acts 11:18).

What might Philip's message have been? Look at Isaiah 53:5–12:

- Our sin was laid to Christ's account (v. 5).

- We are all sinful people (v. 6).

- He voluntarily gave himself for the sin of His people (vv. 7–9).

- He will be vindicated and see the fruit of His work (vv. 10–12).

The Ethiopian's response (Acts 8:36) would indicate that Philip had called upon him to repent and be baptized. We ought not to be paralyzed by God's sovereignty in salvation. **God directs, prepares, and ordains (2 Thessalonians 2:13), but He chooses to bring people to faith through human messengers.** "'Everyone who calls on the name of the Lord will be saved.' How, then, can they call on the one they have not believed in? And how can they believe in the one of whom they have not heard? And how can they hear without someone preaching to them? . . . Consequently, faith comes from hearing the message" (Romans 10:13–14, 17).

God is ever reaching out to people. He sends us out "to fish for people" (Matthew 4:19). He urges us to pray for laborers for the harvest field (Luke 10:2). He sends His Son to be Savior and His Spirit to be cowitness. And He enables us to explain the truth (Acts 8:35; Matthew 28:20).

What caused such rejoicing in the Ethiopian (v. 39)?

Reflect on the ministry of Philip in Acts 8. How will knowing that God is the one who "directs, prepares, and ordains" help you in your outreach efforts?

Day 22

Read Acts 9:1–6

Here is a major turning point in Acts and in the history of the church. It is the conversion of Paul, which Luke repeats in his narrative for emphasis (see Acts 22:6–21; 26:12–18).

Paul never forgets what a zealous persecutor of the church he was (Philippians 3:6; 1 Timothy 1:15–16; 1 Corinthians 15:9). He had authority from the high priest in Jerusalem to arrest followers of the Way in the synagogues of Damascus and take them back to Jerusalem. His experience is much like that of Moses in Exodus 3:2:

- A light, a voice (Acts 9:3–4; Exodus 3:2–4)

- The solemn repetition of the name "Saul, Saul" (Acts 9:4) and "Moses! Moses!" (Exodus 3:4)

Notice that Jesus asks Saul why the latter is persecuting Him (Acts 9:4). Jesus takes persecution of the followers of the Way personally; to persecute them is to persecute Him (see Matthew 10:18–22). One of Saul's first lessons is on the solidarity of the believer and Christ. It is little wonder that the concept of being "in Christ" dominates his teaching. While Jesus questions Saul as to the reason for his zealous persecution, Saul is far more interested in who is addressing him (Acts 9:5). Jesus identifies himself by His earthly name and address (v. 5; 22:8) as the one who in reality is being persecuted by Saul. The Lord Jesus, however, has plans for Saul and tells him to go into Damascus and wait (9:6).

Saul understands the Damascus road experience as his conversion, his seeing of the resurrected Christ (1 Corinthians 9:1; 15:8). **The conversion of such a zealous persecutor as Saul provides further evidence for the truth and power of the gospel to save.** No one could argue that Saul's seeing the resurrected Christ was wishful thinking on his part.

The zealous persecutor becomes the zealous apostle: "Amazing grace, how sweet the sound that saves a wretch like me."

What characteristics has Jesus revealed about himself on the Damascus road?

Why do you think the conversion of Saul is such a major turning point for Luke?

Day 23

Read Acts 9:7–19

Ananias is understandably cautious about his vision (Acts 9:10). The Lord is specific about the direction He gives (v. 11). He has wonderfully prepared the way for Ananias (v. 12).

Ananias knows all about Saul. He does not want to go anywhere near him (vv. 13–14). The Lord is insistent (vv. 15–16). Saul's commissioning as the apostle to the Gentiles is repeated by Paul in each of the accounts of his conversion in Acts 22:21 and 26:17. It is clear that his focus on Gentiles is not exclusive as he begins preaching the divinity of Jesus in the Damascus synagogues (9:20). Whereas Peter required a special vision to be convinced that God has included the Gentiles among His people, there was no such hesitation for Paul. He was a stubborn resister of Christ, but once that resistance was broken, he realized that the gospel was for all.

Along with his partners, he takes the gospel throughout Asia Minor and into Europe, to the synagogues first and then to the fields, the market places, and the lecture halls. He does not hesitate to make clear that Yahweh is no local deity whose promises are for Jews only. Jesus is universal Lord, judgment day is coming, and all people should repent in preparation (17:30–31). What an effect it all has on the hearers!

All conversions are significant, but Paul's is particularly so since it will change the course of history for a major part of the world.

Not long ago, I enjoyed a trip through Europe, where the gospel arrived in the first century after Paul and Barnabas brought it to Philippi (Acts 16). The influence of the Christian faith on the continent's architecture, art galleries, and opera houses was evident. In his commentary on Acts, British preacher Campbell Morgan writes, "Essentially the measure of Europe's freedom is the measure in which she has obeyed the principles of Christianity."[5]

Jesus is for all; wherever the unstoppable gospel goes, it brings about deep transformation in those who accept it.

5. G. Campbell Morgan, *The Acts of the Apostles* (New York: F. H. Revell, 1924).

Think about the model of discipleship provided to us by Ananias.

How does the gospel challenge you in reaching out to your culture?

Read Acts 9:20–31

Saul baffles the Jews in Damascus. They expect him to defend Judaism against the new movement, but now he is preaching that Jesus is the Son of God (Acts 9:20) and proving that Jesus is the Christ (v. 22). Luke tells of their reaction: they are astonished (v. 21) and baffled (v. 22). Meanwhile, Saul grows more and more influential. He cannot be beaten in argument, so the Jews plan to kill him instead (v. 23). Here is another example of unreasoning, blind belligerence.

The reluctance of the believers in Jerusalem to accept Saul was only broken by the encouraging intervention of Barnabas (v. 27). Saul is described as "speaking boldly" (v. 28), and he "talked and debated with the Hellenistic Jews" (v. 29). But again the response is not to recognize his argument but to seek to kill him (v. 29). For his own safety he is sent to his hometown of Tarsus (v. 30).

The following verse (v. 31) is a summary of the life of the church at this time. It is probably about AD 35. The church now has a time of peace. It is free of external threat, strengthened and encouraged by the Holy Spirit, growing numerically, and living in reverence of God. With Saul's conversion, the persecutions that followed the death of Stephen come to an end.

Luke's account of Saul's conversion is now complete. Paul's calling was to take the gospel not only to Jews but also to the Gentile world. He was God's chosen instrument to bring about the spread of the gospel throughout the Roman Empire.

The effects of his conversion are seen starkly in his changed intention; he approaches Damascus to arrest followers of the Way (v. 2), but when he arrives in the city, he preaches that Jesus is God the Son (v. 20).

This gospel, which will turn the world upside down, will first transform its messenger.

Paul's contribution to the Gentile mission was unique, but first he had to experience the revolutionary newness of being in Christ (2 Corinthians 5:17).

The emphasis of Paul's ministry and God's gospel is that at the center of God's purpose is a person: Jesus Christ, the Son of God.

Saul's opposition to Christ is apparent from Acts 7–9. How has Saul changed after he met the risen Christ? How have you changed after you believed in Jesus?

Reflect on the experience of the church in Acts 9:31. What do you think a church "living in the fear of the Lord and encouraged by the Holy Spirit" would look like?

Read Acts 9:32–43

The book of Acts has had many names throughout its life—for example, "The Deeds of the Apostles," "The Acts of All the Apostles," "The Acts of the Holy Spirit," and "What Jesus Continued to Do." Some of these titles seek to express the truth that in the Gospels are the records of what Jesus did in His life on earth, while in Acts we have the record of what Jesus continues to do through His Spirit as He sits at God's right hand.

The account of Peter's raising Dorcas is very similar to the account in Luke 8:49–56 where Jesus raises Jairus's daughter. There is no doubt that both the girl and the woman are dead—the professional mourners for Jairus's daughter have arrived (v. 52), and Dorcas's body has been washed and readied for burial (Acts 9:37). Peter had been with Jesus at the resurrection of Jairus's daughter, and he is so bold as to pray that Jesus would do it again in the case of Dorcas.

A creation miracle is required for resurrection to take place—even if it is not permanent as in the cases of Dorcas and Jairus's daughter. The body's vital processes need to be restored to life. **The fact that so many people trust in the Lord as a result of Dorcas's resurrection (v. 42) underlines not only its reality but also the reality that Jesus continues to work through His servants.**

Why do so many people today find it hard to believe in resurrection? Jesus is Lord of life and death. He has defeated death, and He exercises rule over it as He sees fit (Revelation 1:17–18).

French physicist Blaise Pascal put it like this: "What reason have [atheists] for saying that we cannot rise from the dead? Which is more difficult, to be born, or to be raised from the dead; for what has never been to exist, or for what has been to exist again? Is it more difficult to come into being than to return to it? Custom makes the one seem easy, while unfamiliarity makes the other impossible. But that is a popular way of judging!"[6]

6. Blaise Pascal, *Pensees: Selections* (London: SCM, 1959).

Why do you think it is important that Acts records Jesus's continued activity?

In what ways does Jesus's victory over death encourage you?

Day 26

Read Acts 10:1–23

Again Luke reminds us that God is the sovereign and active evangelist. He is the expansive God, dealing with a people of limited vision—in this case Peter, the foremost apostle to the Jews.

Peter's understanding of what Jesus said in Luke 24:47 has remained limited. As Acts 10 begins, Peter believes God's intention is to bring the gospel not to people of all nations, but to the Jews of all nations.

God first prepares the Gentile Cornelius (vv. 1–8). He is a well-respected Roman centurion who is also a devout God-fearer, which means he worships the God of Israel but has not fully converted to Judaism. Therefore, he is technically still an unclean Gentile. Despite his morality and generosity, he still needs Christian conversion.

Luke reminds us that Peter was staying in the house of a tanner (see 9:43; 10:6; 10:32). As a tanner, Simon worked with animal hides and would be perceived by strict Jews as unclean (Leviticus 5:2; 11:24, 39). Peter staying with him suggests that Peter was not scrupulous in observing Jewish traditions.

Having prepared Cornelius, God now prepares Peter (Acts 10:9–23). He is given a vision of clean and unclean food and told to eat it. Peter replies, "Surely not, Lord!" He has never eaten unclean food.

The lesson for Peter is that the distinction between clean and unclean no longer applies to food or to people (v. 15). This is what Jesus implied when He taught that it is not what enters a man from outside that makes him unclean, but what comes from within (see Mark 7:17–23).

God is preparing Peter to leap an enormous barrier in his thinking. Just as he is reflecting on the vision (Acts 10:17), Peter is told messengers from Cornelius have arrived and that he is to go with them.

God's purpose is that not only Jews but also non-Jews should hear the gospel and be saved. Peter needed to learn that old distinctions about what, or with whom you eat, no longer apply.

Do we believe that people must earn the right to receive the gospel? How might this attitude manifest itself in our evangelism?

As fine a man as Cornelius was, he nevertheless needed the salvation that comes through Jesus Christ. Are there people you are tempted to believe may not need to hear the gospel?

Day 27

Read Acts 10:24–48

God is the great evangelist, who often sets up seemingly coincidental meetings such as that between Philip and the Ethiopian on the Gaza Road. Now He is about to bring Peter and Cornelius together in a ground-breaking, evangelistic encounter.

Peter, the opportunistic evangelist of earlier chapters, seems quite blind to the opportunity he has of preaching to Cornelius and his friends. Here he is a reluctant evangelist (Acts 10:28–29). He still hasn't realized that God's saving purposes could include non-Jews.

When Cornelius tells Peter about God's dealings with him, he finally gets it (vv. 34–35). Peter preaches a three-point sermon that closely follows the overall structure of Mark's gospel (Peter was the primary source of Mark's gospel):

• The exemplary life of Jesus (vv. 37–38)

• The death and resurrection of Jesus, which Peter witnessed (vv. 39–41)

• The coming judgment by Jesus and that forgiveness of sin is through Him (vv. 42–43)

In Acts 2, the Holy Spirit comes before the preaching (vv. 1–4), and in Acts 8, after the preaching (vv. 15–17). Here in Acts 10, He comes during the preaching—before Peter reaches the call to repent (v. 44). God takes control of this evangelistic encounter. In verse 45, the witnesses to this event are called "circumcised believers." The critical point is that the Holy Spirit has fallen on the uncircumcised, without their meeting the prerequisite of baptism or circumcision.

The distinction between clean and unclean people has been removed. Peter stays on with the new Gentile believers for a few days (v. 48). No doubt they ate together. We are not told what was on the menu, but in God's eyes it was all clean, just as all those present were clean because of the peace that comes through Jesus Christ (v. 36).

God is directing Peter to "press beyond the fringe," crossing racial, cultural, and religious boundaries in his evangelistic concerns. In what ways does this section encourage you to reach out?

What does this episode tell you about God's desires or plans for all men (see 1 Timothy 2:3–4)?

Read Acts 11:1–18

News travels quickly. The news of the Holy Spirit's coming on the Gentiles reaches Jerusalem before Peter does. The church there is horrified by reports of Peter mixing with Gentiles (Acts 11:3).

Peter vividly describes what happened, especially the coming of the Holy Spirit upon Cornelius and his household (v. 15), noting he had six witnesses who can testify to the fact (v. 12).

Earlier in Acts, Peter asked the Sanhedrin to judge if it is right to obey them or to obey God (4:19). Here, as Peter tells his Christian Jewish brothers in Jerusalem about the events at Cornelius's house, he applies the same principle. Peter wasn't about to oppose God by denying water baptism (10:47–48) to those whom God had baptized in the Spirit (v. 17).

All objections are dropped (v. 18), and the Jerusalem church praises God that He has given the gift of repentance that leads to life (salvation) to non-Jews.

This is an important turning point in the church's life. Luke indicates its importance by reporting it three times (see Acts 10; 11; 15:1–11).

Luke again shows us people "warts and all." Tanning was considered an unclean activity, and although Luke tells us Peter was staying at Simon the tanner's house, Peter makes no mention of this in his report to his Jewish brothers (11:5). We don't know why he didn't mention it, but we know that to accept hospitality from an unclean Jew was unthinkable. It required a vision from God to change his thinking (10:9–20).

How does the account of the Gentile experience in Acts 11:18 help us in our evangelistic efforts?

Peter was reluctant to share the gospel with Gentiles. How does Acts 10–11 challenge your limited perspective about God's interest in the lost?

Day 29

Read Acts 11:19–30 and 13:1–3

The church at Antioch in Syria, north of Jerusalem, is the mother of almost all Gentile Christian churches. Due to God's work (Acts 11:21), there were many believers there. So the Jerusalem church responds by appointing Barnabas and sending him as their representative to nurture the believers.

With the arrival of Barnabas in Antioch, an even greater number of people are added to the church (v. 24). Luke reports that Barnabas went to Tarsus to find Saul, and Barnabas then took him to Antioch. Then, for a third time, he tells of great numbers of people in Antioch (v. 26).

Barnabas was an encourager (v. 23). Both he and Saul established the church by providing sound teaching for a whole year (v. 26). At Antioch, believers are first called Christians (v. 26), literally, "belonging to Christ."

Luke describes a well-taught church, showing clear evidence of repentance and faith. The church at Antioch:

• Listens to and respects the prophetic word of Agabus (v. 28)

• Responds to the Word with financial generosity (v. 29)

• Is culturally diverse. This is reflected in their leaders, who include Jews, a black African, and a north African (13:1–3)

• Has leaders who are sensitive to the voice of the Holy Spirit (v. 2)

• Generously shares its best personnel (v. 3)

This clearly challenges the mindset that would keep the best for self and let God have the rest.

Again, the expansive purpose of God is at the forefront of events. Luke records that the Holy Spirit said, "Set apart for me Barnabas and Saul for the work to which I have called them" (v. 2). Other similar words of God are recorded in Acts 5:20; 8:26; 9:15; 10:20; 16:9–10; and 18:9–10.

Do you keep the best and share the rest?

How can your church nurture believers in their relationship with God and then send them out to help other churches grow?

Day 30

Read Acts 12

Acts 12 begins so well for Herod. James is decapitated, and Peter is imprisoned. Yet the chapter ends with Peter walking free while Herod is struck down, eaten by worms, and dies (v. 23). Here is evidence of God's hidden hand at work.

Concerning Peter's release, the turning point is verse 5, where we are told the church earnestly prayed to God for Peter.

Luke contrasts Herod's political authority with God's sovereign control.

Peter is very well guarded in prison, but the angel of God delivers him (vv. 6–10). The callous Herod has the soldiers who had been assigned to guard Peter executed (v. 19).

Luke could have omitted verses 12–17, but he doesn't. He deliberately shows the church's unbelief in its own prayers. Their prayer is effective, but their faith imperfect. Their prayer is answered, but those praying themselves find it unbelievable. When we are tempted to have faith in our own prayers or to think that prayer is somehow forcing the hand of a reluctant God, here we see that God is greater than our praying. Here He graciously answers unbelieving prayer.

During the course of his quarrel with the people of Tyre and Sidon, Herod had cut off their food supplies. Notice how they respond to his speech in verse 22. Then Herod is struck down. It is ironic that the one who denied food to Tyre becomes food for worms.

Peter is delivered, Herod is dead, and Luke tells us that the Word of God "continued to spread and flourish" (v. 24). This is an encouraging start to the Gentile mission (v. 25). These radical reversals are evidence that the progress of the gospel is unstoppable.

In what ways are you encouraged by the vitality of the Word of God and its messengers, in contrast to Herod's wormy death?

Dark days come to all of us. How does this chapter provide reassurance in the midst of darkness?

Day 31

Read Acts 13:1–12

Acts is great literature. Great literature has many layers of subtle meaning, and Acts is no exception. Acts 13 sees the beginning of the first missionary journey. **Note how Luke uses the names of people and places to provide emphasis, irony, comparison, and contrast.**

Barnabas and Saul are sent on their way (v. 2). Note that Barnabas is listed before Saul in this verse. This becomes significant as we read of their progress in subsequent chapters.

Their first stop is the island of Cyprus, Barnabas's homeland (see 4:36). As they travel, they move from east to west, and even though the Gentile church has commissioned them, they begin by preaching in the synagogue at each town (13:5).

In Paphos, Cyprus, they meet a Jewish sorcerer, Bar-Jesus (v. 6), a name that literally means "son of Jesus." This man acts as an adviser to the Roman representative, Sergius Paulus. In verse 8, Luke uses the sorcerer's nickname, Elymas, which means "magician." This man is a Jew dabbling in magic, something explicitly forbidden by God's law (see Deuteronomy 18:10–11).

Saul recognizes the sorcerer's true character. He is not a "son of Jesus," but a "child of the devil" (v. 10). The man is struck with blindness. This is the first sign, or miracle, God performs through Saul, and Paul could relate to it. His physical blindness led to his finding spiritual sight. (see 9:8–9).

Sergius is an intelligent man. Upon seeing what happened to his adviser, and having heard the word of God, he believes (13:12).

From this point on in Acts, Luke uses Saul's Roman name, Paul. This is another example of his subtle use of names to convey meaning. In the wider context of Acts, Paul is a more fitting name for the apostle, given that his ministry extended across the Roman world.

In Acts 13, Luke uses the name change to indicate a close connection between the Senate's representative, Sergius Paulus, and God's representative, Paul. Perhaps his intention is to show that Paul is on equal footing with these Roman provincial leaders.

Why do you think
Luke shows such
interest in names
(see Acts 4:36; 11:26;
13:6–7, 9–10)?

Why do you think
the order in which
names is used is
significant (see Acts
13:2, 46; 14:1;
15:2, 12)?

Day 32

Read Acts 13:13–52

The team, now minus John Mark, moves on to Pisidian Antioch and visits the synagogue there.

Paul is now clearly the spokesman (Acts 13:16), and his name precedes Barnabas's in verses 46 and 50. There is no evidence of competition. The order simply reflects the reality of giftedness and leadership. This reminds us of the old saying, "It takes more grace than I can tell, to play the second fiddle well."

Paul now speaks like Stephen as he reviews the history of God's people, Israel. Here he makes the only reference to his namesake, King Saul, in the New Testament (vv. 21–22). Saul's reign is remembered for its lack of regard for God's Word.

Paul says that God has sent the Son of David, the Savior Jesus, and that through Jesus salvation is now available for Jews and God-fearing Gentiles (vv. 16–26).

This Jesus was rejected by His own people, killed, raised from the dead by God, and seen by many witnesses (vv. 27–31).

Stephen did not get this far in his own sermon, being interrupted by the Sanhedrin. Paul, facing a different audience, makes the most of this opportunity to emphasize the resurrection of Jesus as the fulfilment of Psalm 2 (Acts 13:32–37).

What Paul says in verses 38 and 39 also appears in his letters to the Roman and Galatian believers. The law cannot save (v. 39). **It is by faith in this man Jesus, rather than observance of the law, that salvation (vv. 23, 26), good news (v. 32), and forgiveness of sin (vv. 38–39) have come.**

There is a strong note of warning (v. 41), but some did find salvation as they heard God's Word preached by Paul that day (vv. 42–43).

The next week, there is a massive turnout to hear the Word. The Jews, motivated by jealousy, oppose the gospel. So Paul and Barnabas turn their attention to the Gentiles (v. 46).

In a typical summary statement, Luke reports in verses 48–52:

- The wider spread of the gospel to the Gentiles

- Opposition from the Jews

- Rejection of the unbelieving Jews by shaking dust off the feet

- The fullness of joy and the Holy Spirit in the believers

Note how Luke emphasizes that the advancement of the gospel is God's work (v. 48). How are you encouraged as you see God fulfilling His work?

Do you see yourself as God's coworker, bearing a message that is unstoppable?

Day 33

Read Acts 14:1–28

The first missionary journey continues with visits to Iconium (Acts 14:1–7), Lystra, and Derbe (vv. 8–20). The visit to Iconium features bold proclamation of the gospel, signs, and wonders. At Lystra, Paul's first miracle of healing takes place (vv. 8–10).

There are striking parallels in Luke's description of the public emergence of Jesus and Paul:

- Luke 4:1–13: Jesus confronts the devil; Acts 13:4–12: Paul confronts the child of the devil.

- Luke 4:14–30: Jesus preaches in the synagogue and is rejected by the Jews; Acts 13:13–50: Paul preaches in the synagogue, and he, too, is rejected by the Jews.

- Luke 4:38–44; 5:17–26: Jesus heals many, including a paralytic; Acts 14:8–10: Paul heals a paralytic.

Just as the Savior ministers publicly among the Jews, so does His primary representative in the Gentile world. Paul is in solidarity with Jesus and Jesus continues His work through Paul.

There is also a parallel here with Peter's healing of the paralytic (3:1–10). This demonstrates that Paul's apostleship is of the same order as Peter's.

The people of Lystra want to give Paul and Barnabas divine status. The apostles' response (14:14–15) is a clear contrast to Herod's in Acts 12:19–23.

Paul responds to these people, whose lives are dominated by agricultural cycles, with a clear message (14:15–17). First, he insists on the humanness of the messenger. Second, he says that God the creator has shown kindness by giving rain, crops, food, and joy. Third, people should turn from worshiping idols (e.g., Zeus and Hermes), or "worthless things," to the living God (v. 15). Finally, the Gentiles' position before God has changed. Now that the gospel is proclaimed, their past ignorance of God will no longer be tolerated (v. 16; see 17:30).

Once more the unbelieving Jews win over the crowd, and consequently, Paul is stoned and left for dead. Later, Paul and Barnabas retrace their steps to Antioch, encouraging new believers along the way and preparing them for what is to come (14:22).

We must not be unrealistic about the opposition we will face as followers of Christ. Unrealistic expectations always cause doubt. See how Jesus tells the disciples what is ahead of them (John 16:1, 4, 33).

Such warnings are given to us for the same reason as the first Christians in Iconium, Lystra, and Derbe—for "strengthening the disciples and encouraging them [and us] to remain true to the faith" (Acts 14:22).

Prosperity theology is often popular, teaching that following Jesus leads to health and wealth. How do the events of Acts 14:22 challenge this kind of thinking and teaching?

Opposition to the gospel is inevitable. What response is called for in the face of such opposition?

Day 34

Read Acts 15:1–21

This section has been called the centerpiece, the watershed, the turning point of the book of Acts.

This meeting of the church at Jerusalem, known today as the Jerusalem Council, is framed by Paul's first and second missionary journeys. The purpose of this first church council is to consider the nature of the true gospel.

The matter of concern is that some Jewish believers were urging Gentile believers to be circumcised (and by extension to keep the Mosaic law) in order to be saved (Acts 15:1–5). This is the same concern addressed by Paul in his letter to the Galatians. If the church embraced this teaching, Christianity would become a mere sect of Judaism.

Such additions to the gospel, even if thought to be good and helpful, are dangerous. They take our focus away from the sufficiency of Christ's work alone as the means by which we are set right with God.

The debate is recorded in verses 6–12. This is Peter's last appearance in Acts, and he states clearly his conviction: we are saved by grace alone (v. 11). Then Barnabas and Paul share God's authentication of their ministry among the Gentiles through miraculous signs and wonders (v. 12).

James, the Lord's half brother and leader of the Jerusalem church (Galatians 1:19), diplomatically refers to Peter by his Hebrew name, Simon (Acts 15:14), highlighting his Jewish ancestry and implying that since he is "one of us," his words should not be doubted. James then proceeds to quote Amos 9:11–12 from the Greek translation of the Old Testament. In doing so, he provides the scriptural proof that foretells the salvation of Gentiles. He says:

- The restored kingdom of God will include Gentiles (Acts 15:16–17).

- The people of God will include Gentiles (v. 14).

On the basis of what God has done and said, it is concluded there will be no additions to the true gospel. In verses 19–21, we read that a letter is drawn up and the decision is circulated.

Things that go without saying need to be said! **Salvation is by grace alone, through faith alone, in Christ alone. There must be no additions or subtractions to the true gospel.**

This very minute, a sinner who is not circumcised, baptized, or confirmed may come to Jesus and by repentance and faith receive freely, immediately, and forever the forgiveness of sin, the gift of the Holy Spirit. That should lead to a warm reception into God's worldwide family.

Day 35

Read Acts 15:22–16:5

The important letter from the church council at Jerusalem is circulated via Judas and Silas.

The inclusion of sexual immorality (Acts 15:29) among the four things the recipients should avoid is unusual. Surely the other matters—blood, food offered to idols, and the meat of strangled animals—are matters of liberty, which can be avoided for the sake of fellowship with Jewish believers, to whom these would be matters of sensitivity. Sexual immorality, however, is not a matter of liberty. Why is it listed here?

All four are activities associated in some way with pagan religious practices. Therefore, they are no longer appropriate behavior for believers. Here the general word used for sexual immorality (Greek, *porneia*) is best understood to refer to ritual temple prostitution. Therefore, the message is that as believers of the true God, Gentiles are to turn from idolatry and all pagan temple activities, including prostitution.

Two ironic events follow in a chapter that does so much to ensure unity among believers.

First, verses 36–41 tell of the disagreement between Paul and Barnabas over John Mark's leaving the first missionary journey (see 13:13). This is a sad event, yet it leads to good, with two missionary teams being formed to advance the work of the gospel.

Second, in Acts 16:1–5 we read of Paul's request for the uncircumcised Timothy to undergo circumcision, so that the Jews will listen to his preaching. On the surface, this appears to be an ironic request. But Paul has his reasons. He resists circumcision when it is imposed as a necessity for salvation. However, when there is no such demand and it serves to facilitate the gospel's acceptance, Paul has Timothy circumcised. After all, it is a neutral surgical act.

John Newton, the eighteenth-century pastor and hymn writer, said of Paul, "he was a reed in non-essentials—an iron pillar in essentials."[7]

The next time you think of "timid" Timothy, remember his ready submission in this matter at about the age of twenty.

7. John Newton, quoted in John Stott, *Acts: Seeing the Spirit at Work* (Nottingham: InterVarsity, 2008), 67.

What does Acts
15:1–16:5 teach us
about Paul, Barna-
bas, and Timothy
and their priorities?

Why is Acts 16:5
such an appropriate
conclusion to this
section?

Read Acts 16:6–40

Until now, the gospel has advanced in Gentile territory through the cosmopolitan trading hubs of Asia Minor, the region we know as modern-day Turkey. Now the missionaries go to Europe (Macedonia) and the great intellectual centers of Greek philosophy.

Initially, Paul plans to visit northern Asia Minor, but guided by God, he has a vision of a man from Europe calling him to come and help (Acts 16:9). **This was God's call for work to begin in Europe, and the first city Paul and his team visit is Philippi.**

The absence of a synagogue implies that this is a fully Gentile city, and the team knows they will find Jews and God-fearers meeting by the river instead. They find just such a group, composed mainly of women, and Lydia becomes the first European convert—God is active here (v. 14). Lydia is baptized and extends hospitality to the missionaries.

The removal of the evil spirit from the fortune-telling slave girl (vv. 16–18) and her discernment of who Paul and his team are (v. 17) leads to the first opposition in Europe, and it arises for commercial reasons (v. 19).

Paul and Silas are flogged and imprisoned. The gospel seems to have hit a brick wall. But no—there is an earthquake, the chains of all the prisoners are loosened, but none of them escape (vv. 26-28).

The slave girl earlier said, "These men . . . are telling you the way to be saved" (v. 17). Now the jailer asks, "What must I do to be saved?" (v. 30). He is told he will be saved if he believes in the Lord Jesus Christ (v. 31).

This callous man, who had secured and shackled Paul and Silas in the inner cell, now bathes the wounds he had inflicted (v. 33). He and his family are baptized and "set a meal before them" (v. 34). What a remarkable day for that household!

The first church at Philippi (v. 40) was very diverse—a woman of wealth with her household, the hardened jailer, now transformed, and his household, and some others. Jew and Greek, slave and free, male and female—all one in Christ Jesus (see also Galatians 3:28).

The next day, after being released, Paul and Silas are asked to leave the city. They do so after encouraging the believers, leaving behind the first church established in Europe.

Paul had been stoned at Lystra and left for dead. Now he has been stripped, beaten, severely flogged, and imprisoned. Beware of glossing over the agonizing pain involved in these experiences too quickly.

What can you learn from the experiences of Paul and his fellow missionaries?

What does this teach you about perseverance in the face of adversity?

Day 37

Read Acts 17:1–15

The gospel now comes to the seaport of Thessalonica. Ancient seaports were infamous for their prosperity and licentiousness.

Here the Jewish opposition seems to be especially tough and persistent; opponents even pursue Paul all the way to Berea (Acts 17:13). The immorality of the city has probably made them more resolute in keeping the Mosaic law.

"On three Sabbath days [Paul] reasoned with them from the Scriptures, explaining and proving" (vv. 2–3) the gospel's truth—the suffering, death, and resurrection of Jesus, the Messiah.

It is important to note that in this difficult environment, it is the same gospel that is powerful. Martyn Lloyd-Jones, after conducting a university mission in Oxford in 1941 said, "There is no greater fallacy than to think that you need a gospel for special types of people."[8]

Jewish opposition is driven by jealousy (v. 5), though the reason they cite is loyalty to Caesar (v. 7). This is just like the opponents in Philippi, who used concern for community as a cover for greed (16:19–21). In the King James Version, verse 5 reads: the Jews gathered "certain lewd fellows of the baser sort" to cause uproar in the city.

After establishing a church in Thessalonica, Paul and his team next travel to Berea, about forty miles away. The Bereans nobly examine the Scriptures in the light of the gospel. They were eager to hear, and many came to believe (17:11–12).

Jews from Thessalonica pursue the missionaries to Berea, and they oppose them there before Paul leaves and is escorted to Athens.

In these three Greek cities, Philippi (see Day 36), Thessalonica, and Berea, we see a consistent pattern—there is a gospel proclamation, a response of faith from some, and opposition from others. God is sovereign. His purpose is not thwarted. He uses the bad response as much as the glad reception to see His purposes fulfilled.

8. D. M. Lloyd-Jones, *Preaching and Preachers* (Grand Rapids, MI: Zondervan, 1972), 130.

To be forewarned is to be forearmed. We should not be surprised when we encounter opposition to the gospel. Why are we so taken aback by opposition to gospel work?

The Bereans were of noble character (v. 11). Note the reason they are described this way. What do you learn from their example?

Day 38

Read Acts 17:16–34

The gospel now comes to Athens, the center of intellectual and philosophical speculation in the ancient world.

Paul is distressed to find the city full of idols (Acts 17:16). The scholarly Luke mentions the Athenians' practice of discussing ideas in the public forum (v. 21).

Paul uses the altar to "An Unknown God" (v. 23) as his point of contact with the Athenians, while reasoning with them at the Areopagus. He identifies God as the creator. Therefore:

- You do not create a place for the creator to live (a temple) (v. 24). Rather, it is God the creator who has made a place for you to live.

- God is not dependent on us. We are dependent on Him (v. 25).

- God is not unknowable. It is we who have strayed away from Him. But He has initiated His plan so we might find Him again (vv. 26–28).

- We are God's offspring. He is not our offspring (v. 29).

At every point, Paul shows the Athenians the futility of idol worship; it minimizes God and maximizes man.

Biblical wisdom is all about living in harmony with reality. The central saying of the Wisdom Literature (Job, Psalms, Proverbs, Song of Songs, and Ecclesiastes) is, "The fear of the LORD is the beginning of wisdom."

Reality is the Lord. To live in harmony with Him is to fear or affectionately revere Him.

At Athens, Paul preaches wisdom. The reality is the day of judgment that God has fixed. The proof of this reality is that God raised the Judge from the dead (v. 31). The resurrection of the Judge means that death was not the end for Him and will not be the end for us. Beyond death there is judgment.

Paul tells them how to harmonize with that reality: they must repent (v. 30). Athenians must end self-rule and revere and serve the One they will meet as judge on the day.

Again, we read of the typical, divided response (vv. 32–34)—some sneered; others made further inquiry; and for Dionysius, Damaris, and others, it was a never-to-be-forgotten day of repentance and new life.

These repentant Athenians had embraced true wisdom by recognizing the reality of the resurrection as proof of the coming day of judgment.

ThinkThrough

Athens was supposed to be a place of knowledge and intellectual stimulation. Yet here Paul finds ignorance of the grossest kind. What do you find especially confronting about Paul's discovery?

Paul shows the members of the Areopagus that their thinking about God was wrong. How much does their thinking match that of the secular mind today?

Day 39

Read Acts 18:1–22

The gospel is "punching above its weight." So far, it has won converts in four European cities, but now it comes to Corinth, the toughest of them all.

Corinth had two harbors and was renowned not only as a place of prosperity but also of idolatry and immorality.

As usual, Paul approaches the Jews first but is again opposed by them (Acts 18:5–6). In response, Paul shakes the dust off his feet as a sign of God's judgment on their hardness of heart (v. 6; see Luke 9:5, Acts 13:51).

The missionaries leave the synagogue and begin preaching to the Gentiles. Although the gospel is rejected by the Jews, it works effectively among the Gentiles (18:7–8). After Corinth, the team leaves for Syria and finally returns to Antioch (vv. 18, 22).

In each city where there is opposition, God used the hostility to open up new areas of endeavor. The missionaries left Philippi, came to Thessalonica, were sent to Berea, were escorted to Athens, and then went out of the synagogue in Corinth into the house of Titius Justus (v. 7). God uses the bad as well as the glad to see His purposes fulfilled.

What keeps the missionaries going in the face of such opposition? Paul was not a loner—he had meaningful and supportive friendships (vv. 1–3). Paul was sustained by the timely arrival of Silas and Timothy and the good news they brought with them (v. 5; see also 1 Thessalonians 3:6). A direct word comes to Paul from God (Acts 18:9–10)—he is not to be anxious or silent, for God has His elect and will call them out through Paul's ministry.

Ministry is always a battle, but there will be a Lydia, a jailer, a Dionysius, a Damaris, a Jason, and many others to encourage us along the way. While bearers of the gospel might fall, God's message is unstoppable, and there will always be others to take up the baton. He buries His messengers, never His message.

Paul's ministry was persuasive (17:4; 18:4), and he keeps persuading, even when imprisoned (28:23–24). The fact of God's sovereign control in the face of fierce opposition means that Paul never backs off in his ministry. Even in his trial before Festus and King Agrippa, Agrippa says to Paul, "Do you think that in such a short time you can persuade me to be a Christian?" (26:28).

Paul persuades as long as he has breath.

What special promise of God encouraged Paul (vv. 9–10)? How does this word encourage you?

Identify how each hindrance of the gospel recorded in these chapters opens up new opportunities for ministry. What does this teach you about God?

Day 40

Read Acts 18:23–20:12

Paul goes on a third missionary journey (Acts 18:23–20:38). The brief report on the ministry at Ephesus, a city well known for practicing sorcery, follows Paul's initial contact there in Acts 18:19. It is sandwiched between two accounts of deficiency—those deficient because of ignorance, the disciples of John (19:1–7), and those who were deficient because of fraudulent imitation, the seven sons of Sceva (vv. 13–20). Some interesting contrasts are found here.

Paul tells the former group about Jesus, urging them to believe. The presence of the Holy Spirit comes upon them when they believe in Jesus (vv. 4–6). The latter group fails in trying to imitate Paul. They cannot have the Spirit's power apart from relationship with Jesus (vv. 13–16).

The evil spirit is not fooled. It knows who the genuine followers of Jesus are. **The Holy Spirit's superior power (1:8) working through the disciples stands in contrast to the powerless, superstitious spirituality of the fraudulent exorcists.**

The resultant destruction of the magic scrolls (words of sorcery) from fear of the Lord stands in sharp contrast with the power and growth of God's Word (19:18–20).

Besides these contrasts, notice that Paul's church planting activities at Ephesus follow a familiar pattern (vv. 8–12). He begins at the synagogue, focusing persuasively on the kingdom of God. Then there arises Jewish opposition. Paul moves elsewhere to teach, proclaiming "the word of God," and God does extraordinary miracles through him.

The Gentile antagonism at Ephesus is both commercially and theologically driven. Paul's insistence that "gods made by human hands are no gods at all" (v. 26) is bad news for the sellers of the silver shrines of Artemis. But Demetrius is also concerned that the goddess's divinity will be stripped away and she will be reduced to nothing (v. 27).

The resultant outcry from the crowd gathered in the theater, thought to hold 24,000 people, leads Luke to record two interesting events. The Jews, fearing blame, push Alexander forward as their spokesman to disassociate themselves from Paul, a fellow Jew. But we will never know what he was going to say because he is drowned out by the crowd when they recognize him as a Jew. Perhaps they think he is there to defend Paul. The city clerk calms everyone down by reminding them of the proper legal channels for action against Paul (vv. 35–41).

Note how the seven sons of Sceva and the evil spirit refer to Jesus in verses 13 and 15. Compare this with how Luke refers to Jesus in verses 13 and 17. What is the unique element in a proper recognition of Jesus?

Day 41

Read Acts 20:13–38

O f all the ministries in Acts, only one is reviewed—that at Ephesus. What Paul did at Ephesus is recorded in Acts 19:8–12. His review of what he did is given in today's reading.

Paul calls together the elders of the church at Ephesus to meet at Miletus, where he can remind them of what they already know. He recounts what he did during the years he spent with them (20:18; see 19:10) so that they can continue in like manner the work he began.

Paul's ministry was Word-based. He speaks of preaching and proclaiming (20:20, 25, 27), teaching (v. 20), declaring, and testifying (vv. 21, 24).

The content of his ministry is "anything that would be helpful" (v. 20), "the good news of God's grace" (v. 24), "the kingdom" (v. 25), and "the whole will of God" (v. 27).

The goal of all this work is to encourage all people to "turn to God in repentance and have faith in our Lord Jesus" (v. 21).

In verses 26–28, Paul uses two pictures to describe his ministry. They are:

• The watchman, who sounds a warning and is therefore innocent of the blood of those who fail to heed it (v. 26; see Ezekiel 33:2–5)

• The shepherd, who must watch himself if he is to effectively guard others (Acts 20:28)

C. H. Spurgeon said in his lectures to his students, "We shall be likely to accomplish most when we are in the best spiritual condition."[9] According to Augustine of Hippo, this type of self-watch consisted of "praying, reading the word and weeping."[10]

Remember, these verses are probably Paul's last face-to-face words with his elders (vv. 25, 38). The elders are to be diligent overseers, with complete confidence in God and His word of grace (v. 32). Ultimately, the flock is His, bought by Him, and is under His protection.

In the twenty-first century world, the weighty is often trivialized and the trivial is exalted. **We must never allow the ministry of serving God's people to be trivialized.**

9. C. H. Spurgeon, *Lectures to My Students* (Grand Rapids, MI: Zondervan, 1980), 7.

10. Augustine, Epistle 21:4.

Think about Paul's apostolic model of ministry. Think about each element of this ministry—the Word; personal integrity; accountability. How would your church benefit from a careful understanding of this section of Acts?

The church at Ephesus does not exist today. In the New Testament, there are two letters addressed to the church at Ephesus: the first is Ephesians; the second is Revelation 2:1–7. In this second letter, what does Jesus hold against the church at Ephesus, and what does He tell them to do?

Day 42

Read Acts 21

Paul has a conviction that he must go to Jerusalem and after that, to Rome (Acts 19:21). He has shared with the Ephesian elders that he is compelled to go to Jerusalem by the Spirit, who also forewarns him of impending persecution and suffering (20:22–23). Both danger and God's protection are going to be Paul's experience.

His friends warn him against entering Jerusalem (21:4). Agabus warns him (vv. 10–11), and his fellow travelers plead with him not to go (v. 12). But Paul persists, suggesting he is ready "to die in Jerusalem for the name of the Lord Jesus" (v. 13).

Just as it was for the Lord Jesus (Luke 18:31–33), Jerusalem will once more prove to be a center of aggressive opposition to the gospel.

We read that thousands of Jews have believed, but they retain their zeal for the law (Acts 21:20). Rumors abound that Paul disregards the Old Testament law (v. 21). Anticipating trouble, James urges Paul to join the purification rites of four men in the temple. As is evidenced in the case of Timothy's circumcision (16:3), Paul did not object to observing the law in cases where no gospel issue was involved. It may have been the outworking of 1 Corinthians 9:19–20.

Professor E. M. Blaiklock comments on these events: "He sought to love, to understand, to act in selfless humility. The result, by that tragic irony which Heaven sometimes permits, was apparent disaster."[11]

Because of unfounded accusations by certain Jews from Asia Minor, Paul is set upon by a mob when he goes to the temple to deal with matters concerning the purification rites (Acts 21:27–31). Wisely, the Romans have placed their barracks near the temple, and the garrison is on hand to rescue Paul from his own people and a premature death. This rescue, God's protection of Paul, is the first of four. The others are recorded in Acts 22:2 and 23:10, 20–21, and 31.

Paul is rescued from a hopeless situation—and imminent death—four times by an unlikely ally: the Roman commander stationed in Jerusalem. The original word spoken to Ananias in Acts 9:15–16 is about to be fulfilled, for Paul will later be sent to Felix the governor in Caesarea (Acts 23).

God can be trusted to protect His workers and church as they proclaim the good news in this world.

11. E. M. Blaiklock, *The Acts of the Apostles: A Historical Commentary*, Tyndale Commentaries on the New Testament (London: Tyndale, 1959), 172.

Paul listened to Agabus before (Acts 11:27–30). Why doesn't he do so now?

In Romans 15:31, Paul asks the church to pray that he will be delivered from the unbelievers in Judea. Here we see that he is indeed delivered from unbelievers—by other unbelievers. Is there a lesson here about how God answers prayer?

Day 43

Read Acts 22

Having been rescued from the mob, Paul gives his testimony in Aramaic, the heart language of the people (Acts 22:1–21). He addresses and identifies with them respectfully, "Brothers and fathers," and tells them of his own Jewish heritage and training. They listen respectfully until he says that God has appointed him to minister to the Gentiles (v. 21). **He asserts that "the God of our ancestors" (v. 14) has purposed that by Jesus alone, without embracing Judaism and the Mosaic law, the Gentiles—the unclean and "far away" nations, outsiders in His kingdom— can be saved.**

The commander of the Roman barracks at Jerusalem makes two mistakes. First, in Acts 21:38, he mistakes Paul for an Egyptian terrorist—a self-proclaimed prophet—who recently led a revolt against Roman rule. Paul's request in polished Greek destroys this assumption (v. 37), for the Egyptian terrorist probably could not speak Greek.

Second, having rescued Paul, he orders Paul to be flogged in order to extract information from him (22:24). As in Philippi, so in Jerusalem, the flogging of a Roman citizen is illegal, so Paul calls upon his rights as a citizen. All Roman citizens had to be treated according to proper legal processes.

Meanwhile, where now are the thousands who believe and are zealous for the law that we read of in Acts 21? Where now are James and the elders?

Paul is left to face the hostility alone. He later testifies that although man might abandon him in his trials, "the Lord stood at my side and gave me strength" (2 Timothy 4:17).

What a sight this must have been— Paul being beaten up by his own countrymen on the steps of the barracks.

Having been beaten, Paul is rescued from the angry crowd and taken to be flogged. We might wonder: will he survive? Will God's plans be thwarted by such aggression?

Tension mounts at the end of the chapter, as the Roman commander summons the Sanhedrin and brings Paul before them (Acts 22:30).

John Wesley said that having narrow interests is always the enemy of the gospel. Why do you think the crowd was so upset in verse 22?

Paul is well qualified to reach the Jews (vv. 3–4), but God sends him to the Gentiles instead. What lesson can we learn about using our spiritual gifts in His service?

Day 44

Read Acts 23

Like Jesus before him (John 18:22), Paul is struck on the face by his opponents. Also like Jesus, his words should not have warranted such a response.

Luke draws a contrast between the Roman authorities, who treat Paul fairly, and the Jewish authorities, who break their own laws. By striking Paul before he presents his case, the high priest has predetermined Paul's guilt in violation of Jewish law, which presumes innocence until proven otherwise.

Realizing that he will not get a fair hearing, Paul divides the jury by claiming that he is being opposed because he maintains the Pharisees' position on the resurrection (Acts 23:6). Once again, the meeting erupts into chaos—this time because of disagreement between the Pharisees and the rival Sadducees, who hold opposing convictions (v. 8).

Paul's tactic works, but he is in danger of being torn to pieces and has to be rescued once again (v. 10).

Verse 11 contains a wonderfully kind reassurance from God—that no matter how dark things look, Paul will testify in Rome. After all, the Lord's word to Ananias is yet to be fulfilled—that Paul will carry Christ's name before the Gentile kings (9:15).

Even after God's assurance, Paul's troubles continue to escalate. Forty men plot to kill him (23:12–15). Learning about the plot, the commander assembles an extraordinary detachment of soldiers to guard Paul and transport him safely from Jerusalem to Caesarea that very night (v. 23). Jewish opposition is not underestimated, and Paul's case is treated with the utmost urgency by the Roman authorities. The irony is that the Roman pagans become deliverers of God's apostle from the hands of God's ancient people.

The Word of God is authoritative and will be fulfilled. As such, Paul is neither fearful nor uncertain. Paul's perseverance is fed by his trust in God to see His purposes fulfilled. The word "must" in verse 11 is translated from a little Greek word, *dei*, which means "it must happen." It is one of the most common words used in Acts, and it appears over forty times in Luke and Acts. God's word will not return empty-handed.

Again, the gospel and its messenger prevail in the face of insurmountable odds.

Acts 23:11 records a direct message from God to Paul. Others like this are recorded in Acts 8:26; 9:6 and 15; 10:19–20; 13:2; 16:9; 18:9–10; 20:22; and 27:24. What do these records tell you about the nature of God and His purposes?

Day 45

Read Acts 24

Having stood before the crowd in Jerusalem (Acts 22) and before the Sanhedrin (Acts 23), Paul now comes before a Roman tribunal at Caesarea, led by the Roman governor, Felix.

In Acts, we read that Paul made five separate defenses before various authorities on his way to Rome. This is the third.

Paul's primary purpose is not to prove his innocence—although that is what transpires—but to persuade his audience that Jesus's resurrection and Paul's mission to the Gentiles are consistent with God's revelation to the Jews in the Old Testament (see 24:21; 26:7–8, 23; 28:28).

Paul's Jewish accusers—the high priest Ananias, some elders, and the lawyer Tertullus (Acts 24:1)—charge him with being a troublemaker, a ringleader of the Nazarenes, and a desecrator of the temple (vv. 5–6). Tertullus's elaborate introduction (vv. 2–4) stands in contrast to Paul's (v. 10). Paul denies the charges of

troublemaking and desecration (v. 12). He does not deny being a part of the Nazarene sect, officially unrecognized by Rome; however, he calls it "the Way" (v. 14).

Seeing an opportunity to grant the Jewish leadership a political favor, Felix defers his decision (v. 27).

Drusilla (vv. 24–26) is the daughter of Herod Agrippa I who earlier in Acts was recorded as eaten by worms (12:23). She is Felix's third wife. He persuaded her to leave her husband and join him.

Felix seems to be tantalized by Paul's preaching. Luke tells us he was hoping for the offer of a bribe from Paul (v. 26). Paul's preaching was about righteousness, self-control, and judgment (v. 25). Felix and Drusilla needed to realize that if they came to Christ, they would be fundamentally changed.

Again, Luke reminds us that Paul is driven by his conviction of the reality of the resurrection of the dead (vv. 15, 21).

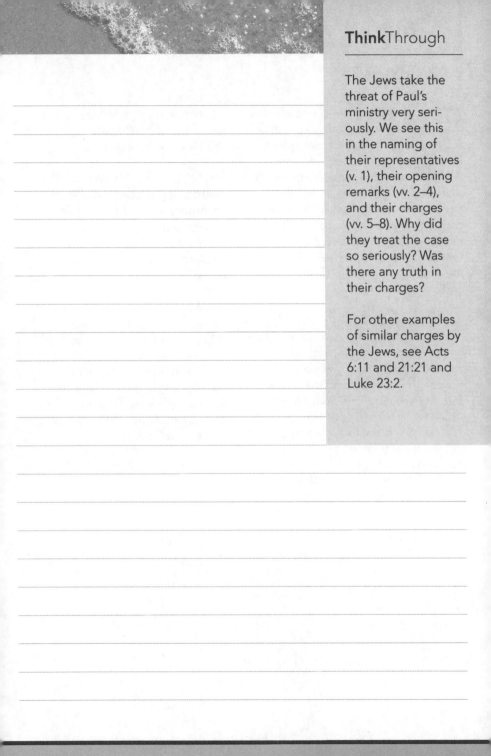

The Jews take the threat of Paul's ministry very seriously. We see this in the naming of their representatives (v. 1), their opening remarks (vv. 2–4), and their charges (vv. 5–8). Why did they treat the case so seriously? Was there any truth in their charges?

For other examples of similar charges by the Jews, see Acts 6:11 and 21:21 and Luke 23:2.

Day 46

Read Acts 25

The Jewish antagonism toward Paul is persistent. They urgently request (Acts 25:3) the new Roman governor Festus to have Paul transferred to Jerusalem for trial, intending to ambush and kill him along the way. Festus, however, comes to Caesarea where Paul is being held, and Paul defends himself before authority again (v. 8)—denying the charges of illegality, desecration, and treason.

Because Festus, like Felix before him, desires to please the Jews, Paul has no confidence in the new governor's impartiality, particularly when Festus naively proposes holding the trial in Jerusalem, where Paul's opponents are strongest. Instead, Paul claims his right as a Roman citizen to appeal to Caesar (v. 11). That right must be respected. Relieved of his responsibility for Paul's case, Festus is more than happy to accede. Here Paul claims his citizenship rights when, as far as he can see, to do so would be to further the witness of the gospel.

In Acts, Luke shows us the solidarity between Jesus's ministry and that of His apostles. Jesus heals a paralytic, and so do Peter and Paul (3:1–10; 14:8–10). Jesus raises the dead, and so do Peter and Paul (9:36–42; 20:7–12).

In Luke, Jesus is declared innocent three times: twice by Pilate (23:4, 14) and once by Herod (23:15). Paul has been declared innocent by Roman commander Claudius Lysias (Acts 23:29); Festus declares him innocent in his report to Agrippa (25:25); and Agrippa will soon add his agreement (26:32).

Think about these two quotes from John Calvin in light of today's reading:

"The more brightly the light of doctrine shines, so as to press more closely on wicked men, they are driven to a greater pitch of madness."[12]

"No man is fit to preach the gospel, seeing the whole world is set against it, save only he which is armed to suffer."[13]

12. John Calvin, *Commentary on a Harmony of the Evangelists, Matthew, Mark, and Luke,* trans. William Pringle (Edinburgh: Calvin Translation Society, 1845), II:159.
13. John Calvin, *Commentary on Acts 9,* Christian Classics Ethereal Library, accessed May 2, 2018, http://www.ccel.org/study/Acts_9.

Day 47

Read Acts 26

Governor Festus sees, in the visit of King Agrippa and his wife Bernice, an opportunity for advice on Paul's case. He candidly admits that he "was at a loss how to investigate such matters" (Acts 25:20).

Festus must send a covering letter with Paul to Rome, specifying the charges against him. He would appreciate input from the Herodian king, Agrippa, who is the son of Herod Agrippa I and the brother of Drusilla, mentioned in Acts 24. Agrippa is said to be an expert in Jewish affairs and the Scriptures.

This opens the way for Paul to present his testimony a second time as recorded in Acts, albeit a fuller account than previously (Acts 22).

Festus interrupts the speech at Paul's mention of the resurrection of the dead (26:23–24). In Jerusalem, the crowd had stopped Paul when he claimed that by Jesus alone, without embracing Judaism and the Mosaic law, the Gentiles can be saved (22:21). Here he has already moved past this point of his testimony (26:17–18).

On this occasion, the unbelieving Festus stops Paul and doesn't engage in debate (v. 24), but he states that Paul is insane because of his insistence on the resurrection.

Paul responds by claiming that what he is saying is both "true and reasonable" (v. 25) and appeals to Agrippa's greater familiarity, as a Jewish leader, with these things (v. 26). Aggressive, unbelieving opponents are never a match for Spirit-empowered testimony. We are evidence of that.

Agrippa recognizes Paul's persuasive intent and tries to dismiss his challenge (v. 28). Paul openly responds—"I pray to God that not only you but all who are listening to me today may become what I am, except for these chains" (v. 29).

Paul says in Romans 10:9, "If you declare with your mouth, 'Jesus is Lord,' and believe in your heart that God raised him from the dead, you will be saved."

Here Paul asserts the centrality of the resurrection and speaks to the closed-minded nonbeliever—"Why should any of you consider it incredible that God raises the dead?" (Acts 26:8).

All along the way, Paul's obedience to his calling was costly (vv. 16–18). He is compelled by the love of Christ (2 Corinthians 5:14–15). Are you compelled in this way? Does your obedience cost you?

Read Acts 27

Through many dangers, toils, and snares, having faced arrest, opposition, and riots, Paul now faces a natural catastrophe.

Escorted by a centurion named Julius, Paul and his companions board a ship to Italy. It is late in the sailing season and dangerous to travel (Acts 27:9), but Paul's warning is disregarded (v. 10). Instead, Julius listens to the owner of the ship and sets sail (v. 11).

A great storm hits and batters the ship. Luke the eyewitness says, "We finally gave up all hope of being saved" (v. 20).

Paul now takes the lead. God spoke to him directly in Acts 18:9–10. Now an angel appears to him (27:23). Though hazy on the details, Paul confidently reassures everyone that the ship will run aground (v. 26) but none will be lost (v. 24). They must stay with the ship in order to be saved (v. 31).

Luke tells us the exact number of people on board: 276 (v. 37). The ship is wrecked (v. 41), but all are kept safe (vv. 43–44).

We see both parallels and contrasts between these events and the experience of Jonah. Jonah disobeys God, but Paul is obedient to the Word of God. Jonah escapes to sea, but Paul takes to sea. Jonah knows the only hope is for him to leave the ship, and the crew reluctantly throw him into the sea. By contrast, Paul knows the only hope is for all to stay on board—but some of his companions lose hope and try to abandon ship (v. 30). Ultimately, however, the compliance of Jonah's and Paul's fellow travelers ensures their safety in both cases.

Both Jonah and Paul face impossible obstacles. Both are in the company of Gentiles, but God is sovereign and in perfect control. **God sending Paul to the Gentiles is a continuation of what was begun in the past through Jonah. Paul's ministry is not a departure from but an affirmation of God's expressed will for all humanity.**

No raging tempest can thwart God's plan—not even the murderous intent of the panicked soldiers (v. 42), thwarted by Julius (v. 43). As events unfold, Julius's leadership recedes as Paul's becomes more dominant.

John Newton began his career as a sailor on board his father's ship in these same Mediterranean waters. On May 10, 1748, he captained another ship struck by a great storm off the African coast. He later wrote of this experience in the hymn "Amazing Grace," perhaps recalling Paul's experience:

Through many dangers, toils and snares
I have already come:
'Tis grace has brought me safe thus far,
And grace will lead me home.

ThinkThrough

In what ways does verse 25 reveal the key to Paul's steadfastness?

Compare and contrast Paul's demeanor with that of the sailors and the soldiers on board the ship.

Day 49

Read Acts 28:1–16

Paul arrives on Malta, where Luke records that he and his companions are shown unusual kindness (Acts 28:2, 10).

Even though he has emerged as the leader of the sailing party, Paul is not above ordinary tasks, such as collecting firewood (v. 3).

A snake bites Paul, and the Maltese people conclude he must be a murderer, because he has survived the storm, only to die of snakebite. When Paul does not die, the consensus changes and he is thought to be a god. The people venerate him, just as the Lystrans did in Acts 14:11.

This snakebite incident recalls Jesus's promise in Luke 10:19: God said He would protect His disciples of that era and enable them to fulfill His stated purposes.

Paul has an active ministry on Malta—further evidence of his commitment to reach all Gentiles, Greek-speaking or otherwise (Romans 1:14). After three months there, they continue the journey to Rome (Acts 28:11–14).

The ship that brought Paul to Puteoli, the seaport of Rome, sailed under the figurehead of Castor and Pollux on its bow (v. 11). These were the mythical twin sons of Zeus, thought to be protectors of those who sail upon the seas. But Paul and his companions know better.

Yahweh has been Paul's deliverer all through his journey.
Paul now arrives on the coast of Italy under the figurehead of these pagan deities, but his encouragement does not come from these brothers.

On the contrary, as Luke writes in verse 14, "There we found some brothers and sisters." Also at Rome, "The brothers and sisters there . . . traveled as far as the Forum of Appius and the Three Taverns to meet us" (v. 15). Paul was thankful and encouraged by the members of the family of the true God.

We can assume Paul was emotionally and physically exhausted. He took great heart at the sight of these brothers and sisters in Christ, in preparation for whatever awaited him in his appeal to Caesar.

Paul has come through an exhausting storm, a shipwreck, being washed up on a beach, bitten by a viper, and now, he is about to walk from Puteoli to Rome (about 140 miles or 225 kilometers). God's gospel is unstoppable and its messenger, who still has work to do, is also unstoppable. How do these facts affect the way you think about:

• Your life?
• Your ministry?
• Your mission?

Day 50

Read Acts 28:17–31

One of the features of Luke's writing is the significance he attaches to last words. For example, in the introduction to his gospel (Luke 1:1–4) where he addresses Theophilus, the last word in the Greek text, where Luke wants the emphasis to fall, is "certainty." He wants Theophilus to have certainty.

In the Greek text of Acts, the last words are "without hindrance" (28:31). This phrase is used to qualify the participles "proclaimed" and "taught." **Luke wants to emphasize that the proclamation and teaching of the Word of God continues unhindered.**

The Word of God has come to Rome. We know from Romans 15:20 that Paul's ambition was to take the gospel where Christ is not known—to take it as far west as he thought he could go, to Spain (v. 24).

Paul makes it clear that he bears no ill will toward his own people. Rather, it is because of his steadfast commitment to the hope of Israel that he is in chains (Acts 28:20).

The Jews at Rome have not received any bad reports against Paul (v. 21). However, they know that many people are speaking against the Christian sect (v. 22). Although some are convinced, others reject Paul's

testimony. Again the consistency of Paul's persuasive ministry (v. 23) is matched by the Jews' consistently obstinate response (vv. 24–25). Paul warns them about a hardened non-response to the gospel by quoting from the Greek translation of Isaiah 6:9–10 (Acts 28:26–27).

Here, at the end of Acts, the gospel has reached Rome as God said it would. Did Paul make his appeal to Caesar? Was he released? Did he get to Spain?

Biblical scholar F. F. Bruce writes, "Luke has reached the objective of his history by bringing Paul to Rome, where he enjoys complete liberty to preach the gospel, under the eyes of the imperial guard. The programme mapped out in [Acts] 1:8 has been carried through!"[14]

In the same vein, Bible teacher David Gooding writes, "But at the point where Luke laid down his pen, Paul—though in chains—and the gospel of God's kingly rule were irrepressibly surging ahead without let up or hindrance in spite of human opposition or nature's storms."[15]

14. F. F. Bruce, *Commentary on the Greek Text of Acts* (Grand Rapids, MI: Eerdmans, 1988), 543.

15. David Gooding, *True to the Faith: Charting the Course through the Acts of the Apostles* (Grand Rapids, MI: Gospel Folio, 1995), 371.

At the end of his commentary on Acts 1:8, Professor E. M. Blaiklock sums up the book in this way: "To press beyond the fringe is always sound policy, provided it is done with vigour and devotion."[16] How does Acts encourage you to press beyond the fringe?

Will you do it with vigor and devotion?

16. Blaiklock, *The Acts of the Apostles*, 50.

Spread the Word
by Doing One Thing.

- Give a copy of this book as a gift.
- Share the QR code link via your social media.
- Write a review of this book on your blog, favorite bookseller's website, or at ODB.org/store.
- Recommend this book to your church, small group, or book club.

Connect with us. 🅕 🅞 🐦

Our Daily Bread Publishing
PO Box 3566, Grand Rapids, MI 49501, USA
Email: books@odb.org